Simón Bolívar

LATIN AMERICAN SILHOUETTES

Series Editor: William H. Beezley and Judith Ewell

Recent Titles in the Series

For a complete listing of titles, visit www.rowmanlittlefield.com/series.

Simón Bolívar

Venezuelan Rebel, American Revolutionary

Lester D. Langley

ROWMAN & LITTLEFIELD PUBLISHERS, INC.
Lanham • Boulder • New York • Toronto • Plymouth, UK

ROWMAN & LITTLEFIELD PUBLISHERS, INC.

Published in the United States of America
by Rowman & Littlefield Publishers, Inc.
A wholly owned subsidiary of The Rowman & Littlefield Publishing Group, Inc.
4501 Forbes Boulevard, Suite 200, Lanham, Maryland 20706
www.rowmanlittlefield.com

Estover Road, Plymouth PL6 7PY, United Kingdom

Copyright © 2009 by Rowman & Littlefield Publishers, Inc.
The map on p. xxvi is courtesy of Red Lion Prints © Thames & Hudson Ltd., London.

British Library Cataloguing in Publication Information Available

Library of Congress Cataloging-in-Publication Data

Langley, Lester D.
  Simón Bolívar : Venezuelan rebel, American revolutionary / Lester D. Langley.
    p. cm. — (Latin American silhouettes)
  Includes bibliographical references and index.
  ISBN-13: 978-0-7425-3752-1 (cloth : alk. paper)
  ISBN-10: 0-7425-3752-8 (cloth : alk. paper)
  ISBN-13: 978-0-7425-6655-2 (electronic)
  ISBN-10: 0-7425-6655-2 (electronic)
  1. Bolívar, Simón, 1783–1830. 2. South America—History—Wars of Independence,
1806–1830. 3. Revolutionaries—South America—Biography. 4. Heads of state—South
America—Biography. I. Title.
  F2235.3.L26 2009
  980'.02092—dc22
  [B]
                                                            2008041868

Printed in the United States of America

♾ ™ The paper used in this publication meets the minimum requirements of
American National Standard for Information Sciences—Permanence of Paper
for Printed Library Materials, ANSI/NISO Z39.48-1992.

For my grandson,
Sean Noah Langley,
who possesses all the admirable and endearing qualities
of the young Simón Bolívar.

Contents

~

Preface

Washington, DC, is a city of monuments and statues, but perhaps the most breathtaking is a 555-foot-high masonry obelisk, a tribute to George Washington, the first president of the first independent state of the Americas. Conceived in the mid-1830s when stories about the Revolution and his presidency were familiar topics, the monument remained an unfinished structure for almost fifty years. In that tumultuous span, the union he had labored so strenuously to safeguard had split into two seemingly irreconcilable sections and then collapsed in civil war. Washington had feared such a war might happen and certainly would have admired Abraham Lincoln's resolve in restoring the union, but as the presiding figure at the Constitutional Convention in 1787 and the nation's first president, he would have understood why Confederate leaders invoked his name in defense of their cause. He remained a Virginian until the day he died.

Within easy walking distance of the Washington Monument, in a small triangle of land near the Art Museum of the Americas, stands a twenty-seven-foot-high statue of a warrior with an upraised sword, a memorial to the most famous and most controversial military and political figure of the Spanish-American independence wars, Simón Bolívar. A gift of the government of Venezuela (now the Bolivarian Republic of Venezuela), the statue is but one of several erected in the United States, in Europe, and throughout Latin America to honor the Liberator, a man whose career inspired laudatory tales among North Americans and earned for him the sobriquet "George Washington of South America," an honor he cherished.

An appropriate introduction of the man is a description by his trusted aide, Daniel O'Leary, who met Bolívar in 1818, before the ordeal of war and politics had taken their toll. Bolívar stood five feet six inches tall. A still robust thirty-five-year-old, he retained some of the features others had noticed in the early years of the independence movement—a wrinkled forehead, which O'Leary identified as a "sign of the thinker," black, piercing eyes, sunken cheeks, an unsightly mouth. He took exceptional care of his teeth. His hair was curly and black, and for several years he let it grow long, but when it turned gray he cut it. In these years he had whiskers and a moustache. He was slender with thin legs and hands that a woman might envy. He was cleanly and made a habit of bathing daily. His appetite was good, but he could endure hunger, and he learned to survive on the limited diet of the Venezuelan plainsmen. He exercised regularly and was an expert horseman. He adapted to the rigors of military life. His stamina in the long and arduous campaigns of the wars in Venezuela and New Granada (modern Colombia) became legendary and earned him the nickname Iron Ass, because he spent so many hours in the saddle. He was a good dancer. He read widely, knew French and Italian, and was a good conversationalist. He was trusting but if betrayed could be unforgiving. He valued the press but was angered by attacks on his character.[1]

Today, most North Americans—we in the United States are but a portion of the hemispheric American family—have only a vague knowledge of Bolívar's life, but in the second and third decades of the nineteenth century, his was a familiar name to members of Congress, merchants in U.S. port cities, and especially in the towns of the South. In Venezuela, however, and to a lesser extent in Colombia and even throughout Latin America, the name Simón Bolívar continues today to evoke the most passionate emotions from people of every social level. Both dictators and democrats draw on his political philosophy for guidance or justification for their policies. Socialists cite his thoughts and deeds to articulate a vision of the model society. Priests invoke his name and spirit in their sermons.

As we approach the bicentennial celebration of the Spanish-American wars of independence, Bolívar's political and social views remain timely and relevant. Hemispheric leaders and governments continue to wrestle with those political and social issues he identified as the most fundamental problems confronting his generation—executive power, the role of the state in society, unity and nationhood, and what we call the "social question" but what Bolívar identified as the issue of color. These persistently controversial matters provide the topical configuration I have used to flesh out the man, to situate him in the revolutionary age, and to suggest why the life and thought of Bolívar, not Washington, may be more relevant—both as inspiration and warning—for what the governments and peoples of the Americas confront in the twenty-first century.

I have two goals in this book. The first is to provide the North American student and general reader a succinct account of the life and career of Simón Bolívar, whose role in the Spanish-American wars of independence and in the political life of the new republics is as controversial today as it was in his own time. A parallel task is to explain how contemporary North Americans at every level saw these wars—conflicts that were as different from region to region as they were from their own revolution—and to explain why it was the conflict in Venezuela and the role of Bolívar in the Andean war that inspired both admiration and fear among the people and especially the leaders of the United States from about 1815 until Bolívar's death in 1830.

Traditional accounts of the revolutionary age in the Atlantic world have too often relegated events in the Caribbean and especially in Spanish America to a secondary place in the literature. The implication of such an approach has been to deny Spain and especially Spanish America a rightful place in this experience, a time of profound change in which a generation of Spanish reformers—*liberales*—in Europe and America drew on Enlightenment theory and especially a Hispanic tradition to articulate their vision of a modern, transatlantic Spanish nation, one of inclusivity of all social groups under a constitutional monarchy and a sharing of the political values of representative government. Their goal was not separation or independence as British Americans had defined that word in 1776 but what may properly be described as autonomy or home rule, the coequality of the "kingdoms" of the Spanish Crown. This movement continued after the disintegration of the Spanish monarchy in 1808, and in the following decade and a half of war, insurgency, and guerrilla conflict, would bring about a political revolution in the Hispanic world as profound as that which occurred as a consequence of the American Revolution.

There were, essentially, two strands or trajectories of this political transformation—the first lauded a strong legislative role, a preference for federated forms of government, the rule of law, and civilian control of the military; the second, strengthened by the exigencies of war, favored a strong central government, a strong executive, and a military not only to defend the nation but to preserve domestic order. The first tradition, it is generally conceded, has nurtured the development of representative government, democracy, participation in civic society, and preservation of basic rights in the independent nations of Latin America. In response, some hemispheric leaders (including U.S. presidents) have often invoked the second as a necessary measure in wartime as well as a means of protecting people and property and advancing the national interest. In doing so, it has often been charged, the second has also fostered strongman rule (the *caudillo* tradition), dictatorship, and militarism, among other perceived maladies. Within the Latin American political tradition in the nineteenth century and even into the twentieth century, both traditions have coexisted, often uneasily within the same country.

Where does Bolívar fit in this duality? Given his passion for complete separation and his personal animosity toward Spain, his critique of federalism, his two dictatorships, his often dismissive comments about legislators, his threats of using the military to "secure" the "rights of the people," and his warrior spirit, probably more so in the second tradition. In his evocation of Spanish-American continental unity, in his belief that an independent Spanish America deserved the respect and acceptance of the North Atlantic nations, and in his role in the creation of new states, it can be argued, he deserves a respected place among those identified with the first tradition. From this perspective, Bolívar remains for many Venezuelans, Colombians, and other Latin Americans the heroic figure of the Spanish-American revolutionary era. For some contemporaries and modern critics, however, he represents the disruptive interloper in the grand drama framed by the upheaval in Mexico—where American and European Spaniards united to crush a social revolution and negotiated an independence that recognized their equal status but excluded the masses from any meaningful participation in governance—and that in Buenos Aires, the only movement to survive the fierce royalist counterrevolution of 1814–1816. Without his presence as a central and driving force in the revolutionary cause, Peru's Creole patriots would have been more disposed to negotiate a settlement with their royalist adversaries similar to the one crafted in Mexico in 1821.

In his political behavior, Bolívar more nearly resembled the populist autocrat who justified his defiance of the law on the grounds that he was defending the rights and interests of the people, not on any privileged social status. Regardless of where one stands in interpreting the meaning of the revolutionary age in the Americas and particularly Bolívar's importance, we continue to frame our debates about governance and especially social policy in the ambivalent context in which he viewed the era. In evaluating the salient issues of the continuing debate about the meaning of the revolutionary age in the Americas, only rarely does the role of George Washington evoke controversy.

The place of Bolívar in this debate cannot be so easily exorcised from our historical consciousness. As I make clear in this book, it is Bolívar's character and the angle from which we look at him that hold the key to understanding him. Indeed, despite the anti-U.S. outlook often attributed to him, his bravura, defiance, continental vision, his obsession with unity, and his troublesome experience as commander of slave, *pardo*, and mestizo troops mark him as someone North Americans would have instinctively admired yet thought too daring in his social policy and too arbitrary in his political style. José Martí, the Cuban poet, essayist, and revolutionary who died in the fight for the island's independence in 1895, sketched Bolívar's life and accomplishments in words as laudatory as those often applied to Washington or Jefferson.

My reasons for that assertion go far beyond how Venezuelans see their own history and the role of Bolívar in that history. The life and legacy of Bolívar offer an insight into how we in the United States see our revolutionary experience and our own history and the role of the leader. More than that, his life is a reminder about the distinctions we continue to make about national identity, about ethnic as opposed to civic nationalism, and the lingering if often unfounded doubts about the role of color in determining the loyalty of the individual to the nation. Bolívar represents the obverse face of the proverbial national father, not the leader who, like Washington, offers reassurance by being there, but the heroic figure always on the move and a vibrant, animating spiritual force who speaks to the compelling values of unity and purpose. When we look at him we see not "the other America" but the other face of ourselves, a Venezuelan rebel who became an American revolutionary.

The second and doubtless more challenging goal is to make the case for Bolívar as the most relevant figure of that era, to look at him more from a hemispheric than a transatlantic perspective, and to draw my comparisons of the man with Washington rather than Napoleon. Undeniably, when we consider that several of Bolívar's contemporaries looked upon Bolívar as Napoleonic in his ambition and proverbial obsession with glory, the more apt model of comparison is not the commander of the Continental Army but the diminutive Corsican who altered the course of European history. My choice of Washington as the comparative figure for Bolívar, however, has less to do with the similarities between the two men—they were dramatically unalike in many ways—but as a means of explaining why their careers and the revolutions they led ended so differently. Indeed, as I make clear in the epilogue, the way Bolívar looked upon the struggle for independence, its promise of a new order, and its troublesome consequences may have as much relevance for nineteenth-century U.S. history as for Venezuela and other hemispheric nations that experienced midcentury crises and wars.

In his life and career, we confront what I have termed the Bolívar dilemma, the realization that why you are waging a war or pursuing even laudable goals is of less concern to your followers than how you are fighting that war. It refers to the difficult choices the leaders of a revolutionary cause must make in order to achieve victory and, if successful, the equally tough choices required to maintain the unity and loyalty of followers and confederates. The promise of a rebellion may be the singular reward of power; the promises of a revolution are many, and made to many, and often framed in a rhetoric of "universal truths." In victory there is often the sobering reality that not everyone will share and share alike, or that those who fought for a revolutionary cause will concede the primacy of restoration of traditional rights and privileges. The leader ensnared in such a dilemma can either crack down on naysayers and dissidents in the name of carrying out the will of the people or be devoured by the revolutionary forces he (or she) has unleashed. In either case, to reconfigure an expression from the 1960s, the leader deemed part of the solution becomes part of the problem.

Of all the leaders of the revolutionary age in the Americas, Bolívar's life and career best serve as illustration of that problem. My justification for that judgment and the argument for a hemispheric assessment of the life of Bolívar is woven into the text. But for both the general and academic reader, I offer here a hint, as my students used to say, about where I am coming from. If we view the revolutions in the Americas from a transatlantic perspective and use the benchmark dates of 1775 and 1825, the meaning of that history is fractured through a French revolutionary lens and the comparative assessment is likelier to offer more differences than similarities. From that angle, the American Revolution is a story of a people proud to be Britons but compelled to reclaim their political rights and who, with much-needed assistance, especially from France, obtained their independence and preserved it, albeit not without weathering several difficult political storms. From that perspective, the "social question" (a phrase contemporaries almost never used but modern scholars of the revolutionary age habitually employ) so often identified with both the American and French revolutions revolves about such issues of class conflict and its resolution and civil rights.

When we look at that revolutionary history from a north-south trajectory and project our assessment to the end of the nineteenth century, when Spanish rule ended in Cuba and Puerto Rico, the dynamic refractory lens is not the French but the Haitian revolution, and the social question incorporates not only the dynamic of class differences and civil rights but the far more troublesome matter of ethnic and racial differences and human rights. Just about everything we North Americans presume about the impact and legacy of our revolution on other hemispheric peoples requires qualifications, particularly when we focus on the role of slaves and free people of color in the war. Although the issue of mobilization of slave and free colored troops certainly arose during the American Revolution, their participation in the struggle was not the decisive factor in the winning of independence. For Spanish Americans, particularly in the Bolivarian theater of war, the use of slave and free colored soldiers proved essential for victory. That difference, more than any other factor, explains why our revolutionary experience proved to be of such limited value to Bolívar as a guide on how to achieve victory.

From that second perspective, questions of inclusion and identity in a republican civil society or even in a monarchical political culture with professedly liberal democratic values become far more problematic and more difficult for governments to resolve. In this context, the proverbial social question prompts us to inquire why perceived differences based on color played such a critical role in political and economic thinking in the nineteenth-century hemisphere and, indeed, continue to affect our beliefs about the relationship between government and the individual. And in this way of thinking, to use an idiomatic expression, liberals in both Europe and America could not comprehend the inherent contradiction between Enlightenment values of equality and democracy on the one hand and slavery and identities based on color on the other. Monarchs under siege from social elites demanding equal treatment or greater privileges often sought top-down alliances with "those from below"—what the British called "Tory democracy" in the nineteenth century—but in the process hierarchical societies began to unravel, sometimes violently. In this framework, the contrast between two of the most powerful legacies of revolution—patriotism and nationalism—become more problematical. The patriotic fervor that became the unifying ideal drew its strength from opposition to tyranny, corruption, and despotism, presumably universal republican truths. But nationalism responds to spiritual, cultural, religious, and ethnic and racial dynamics.

Such comparisons are a reminder of the benefits of viewing the life and career of Bolívar in the context of three revolutions—the American, Haitian, and Spanish-American revolutions—and the dynamic linkages fashioned between them. Undeniably, the traditional transatlantic trajectory offers a more convenient and presumably more justifiable means of making comparisons and judgments about the revolutions in the Atlantic world and helps us to better understand how and why the independent nations that came in their wake had differing experiences. But it does not tell us all that much about why the American Revolution brought forth leaders with such fundamentally different character traits and especially differing war tactics and strategies as George Washington and Bolívar, nor does such an approach give sufficient attention to the impact the Haitian and Spanish-American struggles had on the political culture of the United States in the nineteenth century.

This book's subtitle—*Venezuelan Rebel, American Revolutionary*—suggests my approach to and my interpretation of the life and career of Bolívar, a privileged Venezuelan who grew up rebellious, defiant, and frankly ashamed of his Spanish heritage. In his mind, the once powerful and imperial Spain had become a pawn of French politics and influence. Over three centuries, its misrule had ill prepared Spanish Americans for the task of assuming their rightful place in the rapidly changing transatlantic world. More damnable, in Bolívar's mind, was the motherland's tolerance and encouragement of miscegenation, thus leading to a mixed-race species of people in its American kingdoms. That rebellious streak, together with his absorption of radical social and political thought and undeniable ambition, reinforced his conviction that independence, not accommodation or autonomy, was the sole means by which Venezuela—and, by implication, all of Spanish America—would achieve equality with Europeans and its rightful place among the transatlantic community of nations. That goal and the acknowledgment that like-minded Spanish Americans would have to fight for their independence, frankly, did not vary significantly from the attitude George Washington expressed at the Second Continental Congress in 1775 during discussions about resolving the colonial crisis with London. Where the two men differed lay in Bolívar's often uncompromising insistence on the need for a strong executive and regional (and even continental) unity among the very different Spanish American political entities and his decision to mobilize slaves and people of color in his liberating army. Those choices transformed the Venezuelan rebel into the American revolutionary.

I append here a comment about usage. In Bolívar's lifetime, the word "American" (or *americano*) was as common in Spanish America as in the United States. Indeed, North Americans did not apply the description "America" or "Americans" solely to the United States and its peoples until the twentieth century. The reasons for this development are humorous. In the revolutionary era, the United States became the only hemispheric country with no name because the Continental Congress was unable to agree on one. Thus we have appropriated the name America as exclusively ours, but dictionaries ordinarily provide a second definition to denote that America also means "the Americas." In an acknowledgment of the diversity of ethnic groups in the United States, the Library of Congress Authorities Division lists 150 definitions of American, all hyphenates, categories that would have greatly displeased Theodore Roosevelt. The majority of dictionaries in the United States identify American as a citizen of the United States, a resident of North, Central, or South America, or any descendant of one of the pre-Columbian indigenous peoples of the Americas. (Canadians, irritated by comments from their southern neighbors that they are "just like us," will occasionally and defiantly refer to themselves as "not Americans.") Bolívar himself distinguished between the United States and America, by which he meant Spanish America. To avoid confusing the English-speaking reader, I use "North American" to refer to citizens of the United States and "Creole" for Spaniards born in Spanish America.

Ethnic and racial breakdowns present an even more bewildering panoply, especially for those North Americans (and British) who categorize everyone as "black" or "white" with too little consideration or understanding of the vast numbers of "in-between" or "colored" people who fall into neither category and to the continuing frustrations encountered by people of color. Briefly, in Spanish America, the progeny of Spaniard and African led to the designation of mulatto or pardo, and that of Indian and Spaniard to mestizo. The varieties of combinations, of course, could be even more confusing. In colonial Mexico there were fifteen officially recognized ethnic or racial types. Yet in the late eighteenth and early nineteenth century, the meaning of "race" lacked the presumed specificity it acquired in later generations. (The English first used the word to refer to the Irish.) "Color" was a different matter, and the distinction between "black" and "colored" often could be as critical in determining status as that between black and white, even in the pre–Civil War United States.

At the onset of the revolutionary age, few of those who called for dramatic and far-reaching changes in the European empires and domains in the Americas anticipated the impact that the color question would have in the reordering of political and social hierarchies. The French revolution altered the meaning of class relationships, but for Spanish America and particularly for Bolívar, color mattered even more. Further, the experience of the wars of independence in the Americas fundamentally altered the meanings of other key words that I use in this biography—rebel and rebellion, revolutionary and revolution, liberator and liberation, among others. Bolívar first encountered these words in his early years when he came under the influence of tutors. Later in his life, they ceased to be solely abstractions gleaned from the Enlightenment repertory of his reading and became powerful motivating concepts and ideas. The rebel is defiant; the revolutionary seeks to transform not only behavior but thought; and the liberator is a militant crusader. In his tragically abbreviated life, Bolívar fulfilled each of these roles.

A more difficult matter relates to the myriad ways in which the experience of life in the Americas affected not only the habits but particularly the thinking of the British, Europeans, and Africans about the relationship of the individual to the group and to the larger society. More than any of the leaders in the revolutionary age, Bolívar articulated a continental definition of "American." Although the word "Americanization" had yet to appear in contemporary discourse, Bolívar certainly expressed the beliefs and sentiments we identify with that word and he gave them a continental voice. He would have understood what both José Martí and Theodore Roosevelt were getting at when they spoke of the need to discard the older ways of thinking nurtured in European culture in order to bring forth a "new person."

My thanks to the editors and staff at Rowman & Littlefield, particularly Susan McEachern, Janice Braunstein, Carrie Broadwell-Tkach, and her predecessor Jessica Gribble. Naomi Pritchard of Thames and Hudson kindly assisted with permission to use the map of Bolívar's major campaigns. I am indebted as well to the biographers of the Liberator and, especially, to the contributors of the companion volume of this biography, *Simón Bolívar: The Life and Legacy of the Liberator* (Rowman & Littlefield, 2008), which I coedited with David Bushnell. Finally, I am especially appreciative of two others for a close reading of the manuscript: Judith Ewell, a distinguished historian of Venezuela; and Wanda Langley, who has published books on women aviators as well as women in the beauty business.

~

A Simón Bolívar Chronology

1783	July 24. Birth in Caracas
1786	January 19. Death of his father, Juan Vicente Bolívar y Ponte
1791	August. Slave rebellion in French Saint-Domingue
1792	July 6. Death of his mother, María de la Concepción Palacios y Blanco
1795	May. Slave and black worker revolt in Coro province
1797	May. Gual-España conspiracy calls for Venezuelan independence
1799–1802	First trip to Europe
1802	May 26. Marriage to María Teresa Rodríguez del Toro y Alayza
1803	January 22. Death of his spouse
1803	December 1803 to October 1806. Second trip to Europe
1804	January. Haitian independence proclaimed
1807	January 1. Lands in Charleston, SC, for a brief visit to several U.S. cities
1808	Napoleon invades Spain and forces abdication of Spanish king
1810	April 19. Caracas revolutionists install junta in protest against attempt by a de facto government in Spain to assert control over Spanish America
1810	June 6. Bolívar and two others leave for London on a diplomatic mission. They meet with Francisco de Miranda, who favors independence. A separate mission led by Bolívar's brother travels to the United States

1810	December 11. Miranda arrives in Venezuela to lead independence movement
1811	July 5. Venezuelan Congress declares independence
1811	December 21. Venezuelan constitution adopted
1810–1812	The U.S. government sends special agents and consuls to several Spanish-American cities. U.S. intrigue in Spanish East Florida and occupation of West Florida. U.S. forces occupy Amelia Island to oust freebooters
1812	March 26. After a fierce royalist counteroffensive, the earthquake in Venezuela demoralizes patriot adherents
1812	August 27. Miranda decides to surrender and plans to leave Venezuela. Furious, Bolívar arrests him and turns him over to the Spanish. Bolívar himself is arrested but with the assistance of a friendly royalist obtains his freedom. Shortly, he departs for Curaçao and New Granada
1812	December 15. Bolívar issues the Cartagena Manifesto, explaining why the first Venezuelan government collapsed and urging New Granadans to assist him in the liberation of Venezuela
1813	May–August. Bolívar leads the Admirable Campaign from New Granada to Caracas
1813	June 15. Bolívar issues the Decree of War to the Death, which declares that he will spare Americans, even if they are guilty, but will kill Canary Islanders and Spaniards who do not join the patriot movement
1813	August, to September 1814. The second republic, in which Bolívar rules as military dictator, but the government is unable to build a social base among the lower classes
1814	July 7. Bolívar and his adherents abandon Caracas
1815	May 9. Bolívar embarks for Jamaica. Much of Venezuela and New Granada come under royalist control
1815	September 6. Bolívar's Jamaica Letter, a major Bolívar statement of principles and assessment of the Spanish-American condition
1815	December. The U.S. government confirms Luis de Onis as minister plenipotentiary of restored Spanish king Ferdinand VII and formally ends the appointment of consuls to Spanish America. However, it replaces these consuls with informal agents in Venezuela, Buenos Aires, and Chile

1815–1817	Spanish-American patriots become more dependent on U.S. merchants for arms and supplies. Bolívar complains more openly about U.S. "indifference" to the patriot cause
1816	Bolívar solicits support from Haitian president Alexandre Pétion
1816	June 2. Bolívar's decree against slavery
1816	December 28. Returns to Venezuela to renew the struggle
1817	July 17. Angostura surrenders to the patriots and becomes de facto capital of Venezuela
1817	October 10. Decree of distribution of confiscated enemy property to patriot soldiers
1817–1818	Debate in the James Monroe administration and U.S. Congress over U.S. policy toward the Spanish-American insurgency. Bolívar's conduct of the war and his decision to arm slaves become major issues in the debate
1818–1821	War in Venezuela
1819	February 15. Bolívar's Angostura Address, a major statement about the purpose of the war and the Spanish-American condition
1819–1821	Transcontinental Treaty with Spain provides for Florida's annexation to the United States. In a parallel debate within the U.S. Congress over the admission of Missouri as a slave state, opponents point to the creation of Colombia (the union of Venezuela, New Granada, and Ecuador) as an example of the dangers of incorporating black and mulatto people in a republican civil society
1819	August 7. Victory over royalists at Boyacá leads to the retaking of New Granada
1820	November 26. Bolívar signs armistice with General Morillo
1821	May 6–October 24. Congress of Cúcuta adopts centralist constitution
1821	June 24. Victory in battle of Carabobo ensures Venezuelan independence
1821	September 7. Bolívar chosen as first president of Colombia
1822	June 16. Entry of Bolívar into Quito
1822	June. Colombia becomes the first Spanish-American republic to receive U.S. diplomatic recognition
1822	July 27. Interview with the Argentine José de San Martín in Guayaquil about the war in Peru and the Spanish-American

~

Map: The Major Campaigns
of Simón Bolívar

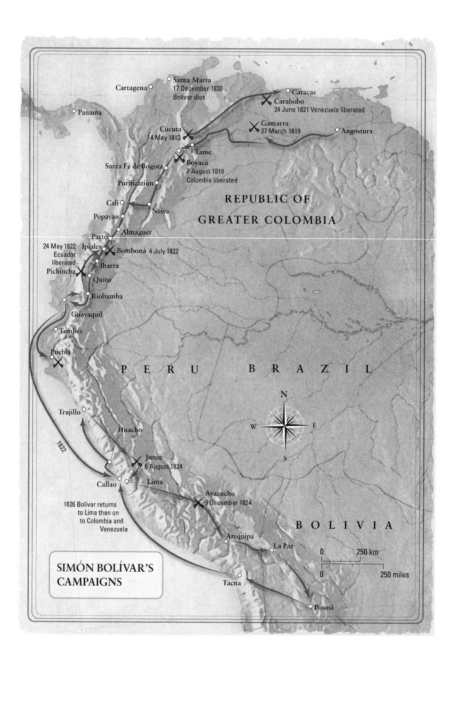

Cartagena ○   ○ Santa Marta
                     17 December 1830
                     Bolívar dies   ○ Caracas
○ Panama   ✗ Carabobo
                                                     24 June 1821 Venezuela liberated

                     Cúcuta   ✗ Gamarra
                     14 May 1813   27 March 1819   ○ Angostura

                          ○ Tame
Santa Fé de Bogota ○   ✗ Boyacá
                          7 August 1819
Purificación   Colombia liberated

Cali ○   REPUBLIC OF
Popayán ○   ○ Neiva   GREATER COLOMBIA
     ○ Almaguer
Pasto ○
24 May 1822 Ipiales ✗ Bombóna 4 July 1822
Ecuador
liberated   ○ Ibarra
Pichincha ✗ ○ Quito

             ○ Riobamba
   Guayaquil ○
     ○ Tumbes   P E R U   B R A Z I L

   Puebla ○
        ✗   N

                                    W ✦ E
Trujillo ○
                                       S
        Huacho ○

              ✗ Junín
                6 August 1824
Callao ○   ○ Lima
                    ✗ Ayacucho
1826 Bolívar returns   9 December 1824
to Lima then on
to Colombia and   B O L I V I A
Venezuela
                      ○ Arequipa   0   250 km
                              ○ La Paz
                                      0   250 miles
SIMÓN BOLÍVAR'S   ○ Tacna
CAMPAIGNS
                                 ○ Potosí

1822

CHAPTER ONE

~

The Preparation

We begin at the end—on December 17, 1830, at the hacienda San Pedro Alejandrino, a few miles from the port village of Santa Marta, Colombia, where Simón Bolívar died a few minutes past one o'clock in the afternoon.

His had been an extraordinary life in an age of extraordinary lives. It was also traumatic and tragic. His father died before he was three; his mother, before he celebrated his ninth birthday. He was educated by tutors. He was a bridegroom at eighteen, a widower at nineteen. At age twenty-six he became a rebel. At some point—the time and place cannot be precisely fixed—he became a revolutionary, although he never fully comprehended what decisions and sacrifices that choice entailed until it was too late. In the final decade of his life he commanded an army that traveled over a territory as expansive as Europe, served as president of Colombia and Bolivia and dictator of Peru, and created an ambitious plan for the unity of the newly independent republics of Spanish America. The descendants of the commander of the Continental Army of the American Revolution proclaimed him as the George Washington of Spanish America.

Few of those triumphs mattered that much in the final few months of his life. In the two years since his narrow escape from an assassination plot in which his vice president and former ally had been implicated, he had concluded that his future lay in exile, perhaps in the country he most admired—England. In May he had set out with a coterie of friends and servants from the fog-bound city of Santafé de Bogotá on a seven-month journey down the Magdalena River to the Caribbean coast. Along the way, his spirits had momentarily revived with news that, as in the past, the populace in the capital were clamoring for his return to save the nation from chaos or, at least, would choose a successor who would fulfill his mandate. The reality, as he must have sensed when he neared the small port village, was that he could never return to power and would not survive the long sea voyage across the Atlantic. In his final days the tuberculosis that had sapped his strength turned his skin a repulsive yellow. At death he weighed less than eighty pounds. He was forty-seven years old.

More than any of the generation of revolutionary leaders in the Americas, he absorbed ideas but was the quintessential man of action. Yet his reflections about his own remarkable career offered little solace and certainly no answer to the myriad questions that troubled him in these hours before his death. It was all so unfair. Twenty years before, when a gaggle of discontented Venezuelan Creoles had insisted that they could claim their inalienable rights within the empire by insisting on what amounted to equal status with European Spaniards (*peninsulares*), he had told them that independence, not autonomy, was the only solution to preserving their liberties, and he had been proved right, or so he believed. In the most desperate days of the struggle following the Spanish counterrevolution, he had insisted that the way to wage war against a Spanish foe who armed the slaves in the cause of the counterrevolution was to create an army of slaves and mixed-race warriors to fight for independence and their freedom, and the patriot cause had triumphed. Throughout the struggle his Creole comrades had warned him that such policies would inevitably bring race war and, as in Haiti, the downfall of his class and the creation of a *pardocracia*—the rule of people of color. And in the last few years, as the political artifice of Colombia—the union of his native Venezuela with New Granada and Ecuador—began to collapse under separatist movements and the outcries against his rule had become increasingly shrill, he had privately lamented, "Those who serve a revolution plough the sea."[1]

Was it his fault that his misfortune was to be hounded from office and forbidden even to return to his beloved Venezuelan homeland? Maybe he had tried to lead a generation too far, too fast. Perhaps he had been too insistent about the perils befalling any political system that sacrificed the unifying power of a strong executive before the unremitting clamor for local control and checks on central authority. Or perhaps his fall from grace could be attributed to resentments over the succession of women in his life—more than thirty-five—from the age of fifteen to his last days in the capital. Others faulted him for his neglect of his executive duties in Bogotá, leaving the day-to-day business of government to his vice president, who so resented and feared his return that some of Bolívar's friends were convinced he was involved in the assassination plot. Others attributed his fall from grace to his tolerance of the separatist movement in his native Venezuela led by his old comrade in arms. The list of complaints was endless, and at this point what remained of this shell of a man was a cruel reversal of fortune: he had not bent and he was broken.

As his mind continued to churn with questions no one around him could or would answer, he kept returning to the judgment of the editor of the prestigious *North American Review* almost a decade before, who wrote that it was not possible to "make Washingtons out of Bolívars." Surely this was unjust. Washington had little comparable education. And at six feet two inches, he stood a half-foot taller than Bolívar, but by the conventional measures of manliness (at least by men), the Virginia aristocrat and commander of the Continental Army was certainly not Bolívar's equal. His favorite reading was not European philosophy but a guide to civility and decent behavior. He was generally disdainful of the militias of New England farmers who served in his command. He lost more battles than he won. And virtually every European government abetted the North American cause, either with troops, loans, or aid.

Undeniably, there were perilous moments for Washington in the seven-year war for North American independence, commencing with the near collapse of the campaign in the first year and the vexing problems of maintaining a fighting force in the face of diminishing public and congressional support, and continuing with more ominous issues of arming slaves and, at the end of the war, the prospect of a military takeover. Throughout, Washington had kept his army intact, insisting on nothing short of victory and independence, and in the last crisis of his command had squelched the incipient rebellion of his disgruntled officers. His return to chair the monumental debates at the Constitutional Convention in 1787 and the overwhelming acknowledgment of his colleagues—many of whom were his superiors in intellect—as the only choice as the nation's first president persuaded his contemporaries and successive generations that, if not the secular saint that nineteenth-century hagiographers imagined, he was undeniably the indispensable man—in war and in peace.

Washington had sacrificed, but in most instances his sacrifices had enhanced either his reputation or his wealth, and for him the demands of war by every measure seemed less overwhelming than those confronted by Bolívar. The length of the struggle, the terrain over which the war was fought, the demands of raising and maintaining a fighting force amid continuing alarms about the arming of slaves, the uncertainties over the role of European nations in the conflict, the waning public support for the cause, the vitality of the counterrevolution, and the perplexities and uncertainties of the early postwar years—all were issues Washington had confronted as well, but for Bolívar they had seemed far more vexing and far less susceptible to solution. As the end neared, he was still reluctant to admit that his choices and not those of his political enemies or an ungrateful people explained why, unlike Washington, he could not return to his plantation home to live out the remainder of his life. Then, in a last flicker of memory before his final breath, his entire life raced before him.

The Troubled Society

Simón Bolívar was born in Caracas on July 24, 1783, the second son and fourth child of Don Juan Vicente Bolívar and Doña María de la Concepción Palacios y Sojo. Six days later, the infant was christened Simón José Antonio de la Santísma Trinidad Bolívar y Palacios.

He was born into a world of wealth and privilege, a child of Venezuela's Creole aristocracy and with ancestral links to the noble families of Spain and Portugal. Over two centuries, a succession of Bolívar male heirs had married and remarried into the richest and most influential families of Venezuela. The Bolívars owned plantations, mines, houses, and chapels. They were active in the civil affairs of the province and generous contributors to the church. And, from all outward appearances, they were loyal subjects of the Spanish Crown. The elder Bolívar had dutifully served as interim governor, judge, and commander of a colonial militia in the defense of the "kingdom" against the perceived British threat in the Caribbean. The center of Venezuelan social and cultural life, Caracas was in the year of Simón's birth a clean and elegant city of 35,000 peopled nestled in a coastal valley. European visitors often commented on its distinctive features. "In no other part of America," wrote the European naturalist Alexander von Humboldt, "has society taken on a more European character. . . . [O]ne feels nearer to Cádiz and the United States than in any part of the New World."[2]

But the Creole masters of the city were a discontented and grumbling lot, none more so, apparently, than Simón's father. An ambitious, boisterous, and pleasure-seeking man—he was in his midforties when he married the fifteen-year-old María—Juan Vicente Bolívar was also intelligent and outspoken in his views about the unwritten but in his mind binding social compact between Venezuela's landholders and the Spanish king. According to a story often retold by Simón, in 1782 Juan Vicente joined two other disaffected Creoles in a written protest about the economic condition of

Venezuela's landed families. Their bitterness echoed that of rebellious Virginia slaveholders a decade before: "We find ourselves in a shameful prison, and are treated even worse than the Negro slaves whose masters trust them more. We have no choice but to throw off this unbearable and disgraceful yoke." The younger Bolívar was in his early twenties when the seditious Creoles found their leader, Francisco de Miranda. Simón sent him the letter with the boastful notation: "At the first sign from you, we are ready to follow you as our leader to the very end, and to shed the last drop of our blood in this great and honorable undertaking."[3]

Where that "honorable undertaking" might lead Venezuela's frustrated Creoles remained unclear. Long a political backwater among the Spanish Crown's overseas kingdoms, Venezuela was a major exporter of cacao and tobacco and had important economic and cultural ties to Europe and the Caribbean. From the mid-eighteenth century on, the importance of these links increased dramatically, as did Creole awareness of their opportunities as well as their vulnerability due to their rapidly changing political, social, and economic circumstances, changes brought on by the intermittent wars between European powers in the Caribbean, the escalating numbers of immigrants from Spain and the Canary Islands, and the impact of the Crown's decision to incorporate larger numbers of mixed-race peoples within the amorphous definition of "nation." In different ways, these and other changes should have provided reassurance of a more prosperous future, but they did not mitigate Creole uncertainties about what lay in store for them. As Humboldt perceptively observed during his six-year migration (1799–1805) through Spanish America, the Creoles (who constituted perhaps one-fourth of the population) were outspokenly jealous of the scant one percent European Spaniards in their midst, yet they were even more fearful of the brown and black castas and their ever-growing numbers. Neither rebellion nor revolution offered a solution.

Their apprehensions about their future and especially their status as the privileged descendants of the conquerors became more apparent when an ambitious Spanish monarch, Carlos III (1759–1788), launched far-reaching imperial and economic changes throughout his American domains. The impact on Venezuela was particularly noticeable. Carlos granted the Caracas Company (a Basque entity) a monopoly on provincial trade and named an intendant to oversea fiscal and economic affairs. In 1777 the Crown appointed a captain-general to exercise military and political authority and a decade later established a high court of justice (the *audiencia*) in Caracas. With these measures and appointments, Venezuela assumed a more important status within the Spanish imperial system, undeniably, but the changes also made the ruling families more conscious of their vulnerability to the expanding reach of the Spanish crown. Spain's second conquest of the Indies had commenced in earnest. In British America, a parallel movement by a king and Parliament to exercise greater control of its fractious Atlantic seaboard colonies and, particularly, to deny its people unhampered access to the potentially lucrative "inland empire" acquired in the victory over France in 1763 brought on a decade of protest, rebellion, and a declaration of independence. And Virginia's slaveholding plantation owners, with George Washington towering over them, were in the thick of the fight.

Venezuela's Creoles were ill disposed to follow that course. Why should they? For three centuries, their presence as the loyal and dutiful agents of a providential Spanish monarchy had ensured the defense and survival of his vast overseas holdings without the need of a large standing army. With the creation of new militia units to defend the empire, the king had to rely on young Creoles to serve as officers. In Virginia, the landed families may have dominated the economic and social life of the colony, but their power and influence paled by comparison with the 650 predominantly Creole families (approximately 4,000 persons) who owned the land and controlled the labor of Venezuela. The racial demographics of the two societies varied greatly. At the end of the eighteenth century, the population of Venezuela numbered fewer than 900,000, only twenty percent of whom were identified as white. In Virginia, contrastingly, whites not only outnumbered Negroes and mulattoes, but on the eve of the American Revolution the great landowners of the colony had already made tentative efforts to persuade poor whites that their freedom and economic advancement depended on slavery and the acknowledgment that both rich and poor whites shared common identifying traits: skin color and the pursuit of wealth. That was a logic that served Virginia's ruling white elites well for almost three-quarters of a century.

The social reality of the American Revolutionary experience, of course, was more complicated, but for Venezuela's ruling *mantuanos* (literally, cape-wearing persons) that was the kind of social readjustment that carried too many risks. Both the numbers of nonwhite peoples and the blurring of racial and social distinctions forecast a different future for the Creoles. At mid-century, Spanish America had ceased being the republic of Spaniards and that of Indians but a society of castes—Spaniards (European and American), mestizos, mulattoes or pardos, Indians (noble and common), African slaves, and blacks. The growth of the mestizo, free black, and pardo population was particularly dramatic. By the end of the century, the numbers of pardos and free blacks outnumbered slaves everywhere in Iberoamerica except for Brazil and Cuba. Spanish practice officially recognized sixteen different permutations of racial and ethnic mixture, but the possible combinations of course exceeded that number.

More and more, people of color enjoyed a limited upward mobility, but the intent of the caste regime was to preserve a racially stratified society. Free blacks and pardos were denied access to the professions, the church, and the university. They could not wear expensive jewelry, were confined to the vilest occupations, and (like Indians) were subject to a head tax. Yet their numbers and their persistent demands for greater inclusion in the nation inevitably blurred racial distinctions, which did not escape a Spanish king alert to using them to curtail the power of the Creoles. Their resentments deepened as the question of social rank in Venezuela related increasingly to color as well as occupation or class. Increasingly, the castas began to penetrate social places and occupations once reserved exclusively for Creoles, in the militia, in the professions, and in the universities. Perhaps the most damnable act in the minds of Venezuelan Creoles was the granting of "certificates of whiteness" (*cédulas de gracias al sacar*) to larger numbers of nonwhites. These certificates had a long and storied purpose as a means of affirming legitimacy of birth to the offspring of unmarried couples and not as a ticket of entry for nonwhites into the universities and professions traditionally reserved for white Creoles. Nonetheless, Venezuela's familial elites felt threatened. Creoles on the 1795 Caracas town council were noticeably incensed: "Only the citizens and natives of America know from birth . . . the immense distance that separates the Whites and the Browns [and] the eminence and superiority of the former, the lowliness and the subjection of the latter." The granting of these certificates, the council averred, would serve only to incite "movements that will scandalize and subvert the order established by the wise Laws that have governed us up until now."[4]

Spanish policies, most Venezuelan Creoles agreed, served not to placate but exacerbate the social and racial tensions in society. They condemned a May 1789 decree spelling out the rights of masters and slaves as yet another example of unwarranted Crown intervention that with other policies heightened expectations of pardos and slaves. Resistance to the law was widespread throughout Venezuela and the Spanish Caribbean, and in 1794 the royal officials suspended its enforcement. Reformers warned that such an act would lead to an insurrection, a judgment presumably confirmed later with the outbreak of a Negro revolt in the sugar plantations of Coro province. The leaders were free blacks who invoked the rhetoric of revolutionary France and insurrectionary French Saint-Domingue, where a revolt by free people of color (some of whom were slaveholders) claiming their rights under revolutionary French laws had led to a slave uprising in August 1791. In the course of only a few years, the destructive fury of the slave rebellion threatened not only the plantation economy but slavery itself and, just as frightening, the fragile social order of those who stood atop the social pyramid. In desperation, white planters invited a British occupying force to shield them. Others began fleeing the island, taking their slaves with them. Some went to other British West Indies islands, more to Cuba, and others to the U.S. South, where they but not their slaves were welcome out of fear of the "incendiary combustion" their presence might create.

Nothing similar to Saint-Domingue's racial makeup or circumstance prevailed in Venezuela, of course, or anywhere else in the slave societies and economies of the New World. The Coro rebels numbered only 150 poorly armed slaves, and the uprising was short-lived and quickly suppressed. But in their brief reign of terror, as had occurred in Saint-Domingue, they ransacked and burned plantations and killed their owners.[5]

The Coro rebellion might have been an omen for Venezuela if the dissident Venezuelan Creoles had understood the nuances of the Saint-Domingue slave uprising. The slave revolt erupted almost spontaneously and in the name of the French king and not in that of the revolution that challenged his authority and would execute him. It had persisted because of the divisions between those occupying the upper strata of Saint-Domingue society. That disunity had offered an opportunity for the rebellion from the underside of society, a rebellion that would ultimately lead to the creation of independent Haiti and the end of slavery in the Caribbean's most prosperous colony. Even the most outspoken Creole slaveholders were able to understand that danger. What they failed to appreciate sufficiently was another lesson bequeathed by the Saint-Domingue upheaval: in the colored revolt, both sides had mobilized the slaves. The whites and coloreds had started the fight, but the slaves—fired with French revolutionary promises in the famous Declaration of the Rights of Man and a powerful commitment to gain their freedom at any cost—determined to finish it. Illiterate slaves not yet Americanized had their own definitions of freedom, the general will, community, and the social compact, and they did not get these from philosophers or political discourse but from their African heritage and experience. This was the "revolution from below" and, contrary to what Jean-Jacques Rousseau had solemnly noted in the *Social Contract*, the Haitian slaves did not find freedom a "difficult morsel to digest."

Young Simón

Bolívar was six when the French Revolution erupted, eight at the time of the slave rebellion in Saint-Domingue. He had reached eleven when the local militias crushed the Coro revolt and authorities executed one of the two leaders, José Leonardo Chirinos (a Negro-Indian mixed blood or *zambo*), and put his severed head in an iron cage atop a pole outside Caracas.

His private world must have seemed just as chaotic and unpredictable to such an impressionable boy. In early 1786, a few months before his third birthday, the elder Bolívar took sick and died, leaving his two sons and two daughters in the care of their young mother, Doña Concepción, a maternal grandfather, and a Cuban wet nurse, Hipólita, whom Simoncito looked upon as both father and mother. From several accounts of his early years, he was intelligent and playful. He was also boisterous, unruly, and headstrong. Many years later, his political enemies noised about stories of the young Bolívar who took mischievous delight in poking the family's slave children with a penknife. His friends and admirers just as quickly denied this and similar tales of youthful tyrannizing of helpless slave children, although the evangelist Charles Wesley had observed similar incidents in Charleston in 1736.

In 1792, nine-year-old Simón suffered another loss when Doña Concepción (aged thirty-three) died of tuberculosis, thus making his grandfather, Don Feliciano Palacios y Sojo, head of the family. Within the year, the old man married off the two sisters (Juana and María Antonia, ages fourteen and fifteen respectively), consigning the two sons to a womanless household. The effect on Simón, writes the Spanish historian Salvador de Madariaga, was profound and lasting. Two women—children of Spain and Africa—occupied a special place in the boy's life and in his memory. The bond with the Cuban nurse was perhaps even stronger than that with his mother. In an anecdote noted by a nineteenth-century biographer, in January 1827, while entering Caracas in a celebratory parade, Bolívar caught sight of Hipólita in the crowd. Spontaneously, he dismounted from his horse and rushed to embrace her.[6]

For almost a decade after his mother's death, Simón's personal world remained virtually devoid of women. At the death of his grandfather, he and his brother Juan Vicente went to live with a bachelor uncle, Carlos Palacios, who looked upon his wards as both a source of money and a nuisance. Palacios grumbled that Simoncito was not only a bother but virtually uncontrollable, a disturbing trait in the minds of the older men in the family. Even before his mother's death, Simón's grandfather had put the boy under the supervision of a domineering tutor, José Sanz, a well-known lawyer and family advisor. After two years, even the determined Sanz gave up on trying to change someone who in our times would be described as a spoiled brat or diagnosed with attention deficit disorder and dosed with biochemical drugs. Simoncito was sent back to the more pleasant and more carefree environment of the Palacios mansion.

What these and similar incidents in the life of the boy portended for the man cannot be easily explained. A child torn from familiar surroundings may be fearful and even rebellious if he or she cannot readily adapt. In Bolívar's case, of course, the explanation is more complicated, and at this point in the story the reader will have to be content with what a psychologist would consider a simplistic comment about the early life of the Liberator. Character is central to identity. It can develop through adaptation and accommodation to a sometimes harsh and insensitive world. Or it can develop through defiance, where the youngster finds solace in reveries and in maturity doggedly persists in a never-ending struggle dreaming of a world others decry as unachievable or a pipe dream.[7]

Despite the emotional battering he endured, Simón's education did not suffer. From an early age he had a succession of tutors, three of whom stood out in his estimation—Andrés Bello, the poet and philologist, who taught him literature and geography; Father Andujar, who created an academy of mathematics in the Bolívar household; and the volatile Simón Carreño (who took his mother's name of Rodríguez), well-traveled and variously described as brilliant and fanatical.

From what we know of these years, it was Bello—who in later years would write the monumental Civil Code for the Chilean government—who believed the young Bolívar was too unfocused, a student who absorbed ideas but had trouble sorting out those of lasting value. It was Rodríguez, the least disciplined and most fervently radical of his trio of mentors, who left the more lasting impression on Bolívar. Rodríguez had read widely in the literature of the eighteenth century, but the Enlightenment tract that most influenced him was the *Social Contract* of Rousseau and its absorbing pleas for a return to nature and, to Rodríguez, its persuasive argument for the strong leader who could intuitively sense the general will of the people. More than any European philosopher, Rousseau stands out for uncommon praise in Bolívar's letters, perhaps because Rousseau believed a nation acquired its identity through confrontation with its foreign enemies and the continuing conflict between the individual citizen's desires and obligations to civil society, one nurturing "economic man" and the other "republican man." In France and, arguably, in the early years of the United States, the ideal was the latter, but in the nineteenth century the political experience in each political culture followed two very different paths.

For his introduction to Rousseau, Bolívar rightfully credited Rodríguez, whose cynicism and irreverence for authority and tradition awed the adolescent in his intellectual and, for a short period, personal care. Certainly, Bolívar never forgot this cranky and idealistic ideologue. Three decades after their parting of the ways, when his power and prestige were at their height, Bolívar got word that Rodríguez planned to return to Venezuela. He scribbled a note to his former mentor: "Come to me [and] you will be enraptured beholding the immense fatherland you will find carved in the rock of despotism by the victorious chisel of the liberators." But the passion of the Liberator's adored mentor had already subsided. Rodríguez lived to his eightieth year and ended his days with a solemn admission: "I, who wanted to make the world a paradise for all, have made it into a hell for myself."[8]

Such self-defamation was nowhere evident in Rodríguez's character when he tutored Simón. If anything, the months of education and training profoundly shook the young man's beliefs in the omniscience and authority of the Spanish monarch. Though he had yet to exhibit the anger and defiance of his father, it was clear that by mid-1796, when Simón reached the age of thirteen, he sympathized more deeply with the disaffected Creoles. In that year the province experienced another political and social shock when three Spanish revolutionaries imprisoned in La Guaira fortress acquired a heroic status among Venezuelan Creoles, who delighted in their stories of Freemasonry and French egalitarianism. With the connivance of a mulatto sergeant, the three escaped, and in the following weeks they joined up with two Creole dissidents (Don Manuel Gual, who belonged to an established family of La Guaira; and Don Joseph María de España, a local magistrate).

The conspirators began to mobilize poor whites and pardos in the cause of liberty, equality, free trade, republican government, and the abolition of slavery, Indian tribute, and most taxes. They called for distribution of land to Indians and social harmony among Venezuela's racial and ethnic groups. The symbolism of the conspirators' insignia—a white, blue, yellow, and red banner, the colors representing whites, mulattoes, blacks, and Indians as well as the principles of equality, liberty, prosperity, and security—evoked the dual spirit of the French Revolution and the antimonarchical Freemasonry movement. The radical nature of the appeal served largely to alienate prospective Creole sympathizers, most of whom were so frightened by the movement that they pledged support to Spanish officials in combating "this infamous and detestable" conspiracy against the social order.[9]

Bolívar's intellectual and personal bonding with Rodríguez might have endured had not the teacher become implicated in the affair and compelled to leave for European exile. Virtually no one in the Bolívar family sympathized with the rebellion, of course. The adult males went even further by signing professions of loyalty to the king and expressing their abhorrence of the mulatto "rabble" and the incendiary egalitarian rhetoric of the conspirators. Simón's feelings about the matter were not so clear-cut. In truth, as Humboldt alertly noted some years later, the Gual-España affair revealed a noticeable generational divide among Venezuelan Creoles. One group remained fearful about the decline of tradition and the weakening of patrimonial privilege; the second was more deeply influenced by new ideas and ways of thinking about society and politics. Bolívar had been born into the first and when he became a fifteen-year-old sublieutenant in the White Volunteer Battalion of Aragua Valley, he was still very much the privileged male of Venezuela's Creole society. As he prepared for the first of his two transatlantic journeys to Europe, he remained unsure of where he belonged in this growing social schism among his fellow Creoles. One thing is certain, however: he was old enough to have experienced the benefits of the society of his birth but not yet alert to the costs of trying to reform it.[10]

The European Venture

Bolívar departed for Spain aboard a Spanish warship, the *San Ildefonso*, in January 1799. A British fleet blockaded Havana harbor, so the ship's captain set sail for the nearest friendly port, Vera Cruz, in New Spain (Mexico). The landing afforded Simón the opportunity to travel overland to Mexico City, the capital of Spain's richest and most populous kingdom in the Americas, and marvel at the city's splendid avenues, parks, architecture, and magnificent cathedrals. By comparison, Caracas was a village. Humboldt had already commenced his classic inquiry into Mexico's vast wealth and glaring social inequities, *Political Essay on the Kingdom of New Spain*. Mexico's Creoles, Bolívar soon learned, were as incensed over their condition as their Venezuelan compatriots but for different reasons. Their notion of reform lay in gaining or increasing their hold on political power and social position against the growing numbers of immigrants, new Spaniards who often treated them disdainfully and challenged them in local politics. In 1794, dissident Creoles plotted to raise an independent kingdom. Five years later, a larger group threatened a revolution that would drive the European Spaniards from the country. Creole hatred of European Spaniards was so intense, wrote the viceroy, that it was "capable of producing fatal results."[11]

Such nuances of disaffection were doubtless not apparent to the fifteen-year-old Bolívar, who befuddled his Mexico City hosts with his outspoken praise for the French Revolution and even the right of independence for Spanish America. But there was little coherence to his thinking about the volatile political ideas of the times, as if he had absorbed a multitude of radical ideas but reflected very little about any of them. In any event, passion, not politics, now dictated his emotions. At the palace of the marquis of Uloapa, situated in the Chapultepec gardens, the animated Simón had a sexual experience with a woman twice his age, María Velasco, nicknamed the Blonde (La Güera). A Mexican chronicler of the times described their brief tryst as a union of "the flame with the stove."[12]

When he at last arrived in Spain in May, his hosts marveled at his charming, angelic face yet were taken aback by his seeming inability to sort out the differing and often conflicting ideas raging within him. His uncle quickly wearied of the task of grooming this young Venezuelan provincial into a Spanish courtier and decided to send him to the home of the Marquis of Ustáriz, a learned Venezuelan then living in the shadow of the royal court. By most reckonings the association with the marquis profoundly influenced Bolívar. Ustáriz introduced him to the ancient philosophers and historians and to contemporary Spanish, French, Italian, and English literature. For the first time in his life, Bolívar began to read deeply, absorbing the great ideas and philosophies of the ages. More than any experience of his early life, writes one of his most admiring biographers, the brief tutelage of the marquis elicited the passion Bolívar often revealed throughout his life for ideas and causes.[13]

The marquis may also have unwittingly served as matchmaker between the seventeen-year-old Simón and María Teresa Josefa Antonia Joaquina Rodríguez de Toro y Alayza, the daughter of a Venezuelan nobleman, Bernardo Rodríguez de Toro. She was twenty months older, gentle and charming, and Simón was smitten. Not yet of age, he wrote a supplicating letter to his family in Venezuela, asking for permission to marry. He astutely reminded the Palacios that if he had no children then his considerable property holdings might very well fall into the hands of another, less favored, member of the family. The warning must have been persuasive because his family readily assented. Before the wedding took place, however, Simón set out for Paris, ostensibly to buy wedding gifts.

Frankly, he was eager to leave Spain, if only for a brief time. He was still upset over a run-in with Spanish authorities in Toledo, where agents of the minister of finance had accosted him for violating the prohibition against wearing too many diamonds without permission. The episode brought back memories of grumblings among his Venezuelan friends about Spanish practices. But the French countryside revived his spirit. The trip was his first personal encounter with a culture and society he had admired from the time Simón Rodríguez had introduced him to the ideas of revolutionary France. For a few weeks, he would savor the beauty and prosperity and republican order of a nation that to him offered such a sharp contrast to monarchical Spain.

But however much he felt a sense of alienation and disaffection from Spain during his visit, he was not yet the revolutionary nor even the rebel. The Spanish sojourn reminded him of his familial roots. His marriage to María Teresa in May 1802 confirmed in him not the power of ideas but of blood and belonging. She was of Caracas and Madrid, a reminder of his Creole and Spanish origins. In 1799 he had arrived in the motherland openly voicing Creole doubts about the Spanish bond. Three years later, he sailed for Caracas and the San Mateo house with his bride, feeling more certain about his future and perhaps even more Spanish than at any time in his tormented and tumultuous life except at the moment of his death almost three decades later.[14]

Such was the judgment of Madariaga, whose insights into Bolívar's character were almost always filtered through a biased Spanish lens. Bolívar admirers and certainly his retinue of cultists generally attest that young Simón's travels in Spain and France only confirmed a steadfast conviction about Spanish backwardness and oppression and his belief of inevitable separation of Spanish America. Bolívar himself offered differing and often contradictory insights about his upbringing, education, and travels in these presumably formative years in his character. He was a complex man, and the boundary between explanation and conjecture about his thoughts and actions has always been a blur.

What we have are clues. But in the continuing debate over Bolívar's thoughts as he entered adulthood, one event may provide a key to understanding the role he would play in Spanish-American history. In January 1803, María Teresa succumbed to a malignant fever. Her death devastated Bolívar, who was now a widower at nineteen. Years later, he reflected about the meaning of her passing: "Had I not become a widower, my life might have been quite different; I should not be now General Bolívar nor the *Libertador*; though I own that my character is not to be content with being mayor of San Mateo."[15]

He vowed never to remarry, which to him demonstrated a fidelity to María Teresa's memory. But he did not elect a life of chastity, as a succession of lovers in his life attests. His passing disinterest in becoming a local official indicated that he possessed not only ambition, a necessary trait for those who command, but sought fame, or at least to be the center of attention. He had not yet mapped out his future, but his wife's untimely death had liberated him from tradition and cut him loose from his past. The symbolic meaning was a blessing but it might also be a curse. He could persuade himself (and those who followed him in battle) that the refusal to remarry after his María's death was a necessary sacrifice for the warrior or someone committed to a noble cause. In this sense, his life became more purposeful and focused. But there can often be another, more somber, meaning to a break with one's past. Often, such an event can lead to frustration and even despair. Undeniably, Bolívar recognized that the loss of his wife so early in their marriage may have given him a sense of purpose, perhaps even a destiny, but he never sensed the personal price he would pay for that transformation—the inability to achieve a harmony or at least a synthesis of heart and mind.

The Second European Venture

The return to Spain in fall 1803 proved to be different than his first visit. After dealing with some business matters in Cádiz, he went to Madrid to console Don Bernardo over the death of his daughter. Conditions in the capital had worsened after the resumption of hostilities between England and France, and food shortages had prompted the government to order nonresidents out of the city.

The following spring Bolívar chose to return to France. One of his hosts, Fanny du Villars, who became a close friend, introduced Bolívar to Europe's most renowned naturalist, Alexander von Humboldt, and other Parisian notables. Humboldt was evidently unimpressed with the brash young Venezuelan visitor. When Bolívar spoke expansively about the "brilliant destiny" of America, Humboldt commented favorably about its future but doubted that the continent had anyone capable of realizing that dream. Bolívar had arrived in Paris in time to witness Napoleon Bonaparte's crowning as emperor. "From that day," he disdainfully remarked, "I regarded him as a hypocritical tyrant," an opinion Bolívar imprudently noised about in several fashionable Parisian salons.[16]

In truth, the impressionable Simón was awed by the compelling persona of Napoleon, who was no taller and similarly driven by ambition and ideology. His censure of Bonaparte's self-coronation, writes one biographer, was a typical Bolivarian calculation, the purpose of which was to persuade his friends and especially his critics that he had no illusions of making himself over into another Napoleon. What Bolívar remembered most vividly from the coronation ceremony was the "universal acclamation" that Napoleon's presence evoked from the crowd. Was this yet another contradiction in his complex personality? He was repulsed by the absolute power conveyed in the act of coronation, but he was doubtless mesmerized by the adulation of the people for the man who was granted that authority.[17]

He remained in Paris for almost a year, then abruptly departed with his former tutor Simón Rodríguez for Italy, a decision prompted mostly by

Bolívar's ever-mounting debts for months of gaming and pleasure. The two arrived in time to witness Napoleon's coronation as king of Lombardy, an event celebrated with an elaborate military parade through the streets of Montechiaro. More and more, his views about the vital differences between Europe and America had apparently become convictions. They were doubtless reinforced by continuing reminders of a small but influential group of European philosophers—the most outspoken was Cornelius de Pauw—who expressed the belief that Europeans born in the New World were inferior and thus could never replicate the achievements of their Old World forebears. Although the story may be apocryphal, it is said that when Thomas Jefferson heard similar remarks at a dinner party during his residence as ambassador to France, he uttered nothing in reply but ended the conversation by the simple expedient of standing up so that all in the room could marvel at his six-foot two-inch frame.

For Bolívar, however, America's Creoles had something far more important to demonstrate, and what they had to prove had just as much to do with their purpose and obligation as it did with their sense of identity and their place in the social order. If there was a movement afoot in Spanish America, as he now sensed, it must have direction and it must have purpose. And, more than anything else, it must have a leader. In mid-August 1805, he stood on Sacred Mount hill outside Rome, marveling at the legacy of a collapsed nation that had "examples for everything" yet lacked any spirit for the "cause of humanity." The liberation of mankind, he was now convinced, could be achieved only in America. At that moment, he appointed himself to realize that dream for Venezuela: "I swear that I will not rest body or soul until I have broken the chains binding us to the will of Spanish might."[18]

The Return

This was a daring boast for a young man of twenty-two who had spent the larger part of his adolescent years far from Venezuela and with limited contact with other Creole malcontents. Nor was there much evidence that the majority of Caracas's Creole families shared his sentiments about the Spanish grip on his native Venezuela. After all, Spanish America had benefited intellectually and, within limits, even economically during the reign of Carlos III. Despite an official censorship, modern ideas about natural rights had circulated through pamphlets, periodicals, social clubs, cafés, and other public places. And, contrary to the prevailing views about Spanish America among northern Europeans, the British, and a goodly number of North Americans, beliefs about popular sovereignty and inherited constitutional rights were as deeply rooted in the Hispanic world as they were among those angry men who gathered at Philadelphia in 1774 to protest the colonial policies of George III and Parliament and reclaim their rights as Englishmen.

Within a year the protest had escalated into rebellion and then a war for independence, a war in which Spain participated, largely to protect its vulnerable northern frontier in the Floridas and to advance its interests and territorial ambitions in North America. For the Spanish Crown, the lesson of the breakdown of the first British empire was both strategic and ideological: A republic borne of revolution must be contained in order to preserve the social and political order. For discontented Spanish-American Creoles, the North American victory offered a different lesson. Revolutionary leaders had mobilized a population in war and effectively maintained their place in the social order. More important, they had managed to preserve and even strengthen the institution of slavery, thus avoiding the twin calamities that had befallen France and French Saint-Domingue in the 1790s. As the Venezuelan Francisco de Miranda, one of several precursors of the Spanish-American rebellion, remarked about the abortive 1797 Gual-España conspiracy: "Two great examples lie before our eyes—the American and the French revolutions. Let us discreetly imitate the first; let us carefully avoid the disastrous effects of the second."[19]

On this critical question—the choice of a revolutionary model—Miranda seemed eminently more prescient than Bolívar and not solely because he was senior by almost a quarter-century. A child of the Enlightenment and a voracious reader, Miranda was both student and practitioner of politics and warfare. He fought for Spain, was a colonel in the Russian army (and, reputedly, one of Catherine the Great's lovers), and commanded French revolutionary forces in the Netherlands. He traveled far more widely in Europe and the United States than Bolívar and knew personally the leaders of Great Britain and the United States.

Miranda was by instinct and training an eighteenth-century man who could not easily adapt to the sometimes harsh and always uncertain consequences of a revolutionary age when ideas about liberty and equality reverberated in societies riven by debates over ethnicity, race, slavery, monarchy, politics, and the social question. His dream of liberating a continent by striking first in his native Venezuela excited liberals on both sides of the Atlantic. In February 1806, in a vessel (the *Leander*) outfitted in New York and manned by a crew of adventurers and mercenaries, he set sail for the Caribbean. Six months later, the *Leander* moored off the Venezuelan coast, and the invaders marched on Coro. After two weeks of random fighting, Miranda elected to abandon the enterprise and sail for Aruba. His flight was an ignominious finale to a campaign doomed from the moment Miranda landed in Venezuela, as a number of prominent Creoles, including Simón's older brother Juan Vicente, joined the white battalion that took up arms against the invaders.

Simón had not yet departed Europe, and, in any case, he was troubled by stories of Miranda's plans to incite a rebellion in Venezuela, a judgment prompted in part by jealousy as well as the far more credible belief that such action was premature. Late in the year, short of funds, he borrowed four hundred francs from a French friend and departed for Hamburg, where he set sail along the north Atlantic route for the United States. Bolívar spent six months in the first republic of the Americas, but there is precious little in his voluminous correspondence and writings about his experience, and his biographers differ about where he went and whom he met. We do know that he left his nephew (Anacleto Clemente) in a boarding school in Philadelphia.

Although his visit to the United States was brief and understandably complicated because of his limited command of English, Bolívar departed with a favorable impression of the young republic, describing it as an example of "rational liberty" (a French term), offering a marked contrast with the English variety and its emphasis on elite dominance of public institutions. The United States, he observed, had crafted not only a new political system but a new morality, a society where the president (Thomas Jefferson) dressed in sober cloth and political leaders spoke openly of education for all and opportunity for the common man—all this without the violence that had ravaged France.[20]

This was in several ways not only an uninformed but a naive view of the early history of first independent state in the Americas and of the Jeffersonian years. The first two decades of U.S. independence reverberated with political bickering, social unrest, and economic uncertainty. Jefferson may have comported himself like a commoner in his dress, but Washington had exhibited all the mannerisms of a "republican monarch." Bolívar's visit occurred when the Washington cult and mythical tales of the Revolution had taken hold of the public imagination. The "inner history" of the revolutionary era and postindependence nation revealed a very different story—a chaotic and turbulent era, especially in the western country, as white settlers granted their loyalty to the new federal government principally in exchange for protection against native peoples. The rational liberty Bolívar perceived thus served as a mask for a nation whose people developed racial preferences even as they became more and more democratic in spirit.[21]

Perhaps Bolívar's unpleasant experience in Europe explained his favorable impression of the young United States. Perhaps he needed a republican model that contrasted with the French example, which had taken a sharp turn to the right. There is little hint of his thinking about the United States during these years. What we do know is that he arrived back in Caracas in June 1807, one month short of his twenty-fourth birthday, and that those who had remembered how he had looked and behaved only four years before—the young husband emotionally stricken by the sudden death of his wife—were taken aback by the change. The wrinkled brow was more pronounced, the black eyes more intense, but more than any physical change was a maturity and confidence that had been missing when he had departed the city on his second voyage to Europe in 1803. To echo a Venezuelan phrase, he had changed so much that "nobody would recognize him."[22]

And, although neither he nor anyone else could have known it, he had lived half his life.

CHAPTER TWO

~

The Rebel

Home again, Bolívar had to be dispirited when he heard stories from his Creole compatriots about Miranda's campaign to liberate Venezuela and the excuses for his failures—the lack of leadership at a critical moment or the ability of Spanish authorities to enlist Creole assistance in defending the country.

Such ruminations about the entire affair served only to deepen Creole apprehensions about their condition and to resurrect old concerns about what they stood to lose if they failed to assert their control over the mixed-race majority of the population, whose loyalty to the Spanish monarch remained strong because the Crown shielded them and, more ominously, because they viewed the Creoles as their persecutors. Miranda found kindred spirits among Creoles when he railed against "oppressive unfeeling government," but they both understood and feared what his rebellion portended for them. For later generations of Venezuelans and Spanish Americans, Miranda was a precursor of independence and nationhood, but for some of Bolívar's generation of Creoles, this "abominable monster" was a prophet of social doom.[1]

Put differently, they had stronger convictions about what they did not want than what they did want. If they had a collective goal, it was neither revolution nor independence but reaffirmation of their political power and social standing in Venezuela, something that could be summed up in a single word—autonomy. Despite their anger, they would not have followed the course chosen by Buenos Aires's Creole elites against British invaders in 1806 and in 1807 when Great Britain was at war with both France and

Spain. Creoles and Spaniards of Buenos Aires agreed on very little about politics, but they shared concerns over the numbers of blacks and mulattoes in their midst. When British forces disembarked, the Spanish viceroy and some of the city's wealthy residents fled into the interior, leaving Buenos Aires virtually defenseless. But those Creoles and Spaniards who remained organized the roaming gangs of *castas* into militias to defend the city. In a second British attack, launched from Montevideo in 1807, these makeshift forces emerged victorious over a 9,000-man British army. Their victory sent the humiliated British scurrying from the La Plata estuary. A decade later, U.S. emissary Henry Brackenridge described local Creole sentiments about these events: "They appeared to awaken as from a dream or rather to be roused into life, from a state of lethargy or stupor."[2]

Had they known the details about what had occurred in Buenos Aires, Venezuela's Creoles might well have empathized with *porteño* Creoles—and, indeed, Creoles elsewhere in Spanish America—who resented the political and economic clout of Spanish families and had begun to articulate a strong regionalist sentiment. Creoles had chafed under putative Spanish administrative and economic reforms that were in some Creole minds a plot designed to transform His Majesty's American kingdoms into colonies. Both had looked warily at the latest wave of immigrants—bureaucrats, merchants, and especially determined young men from the Spanish north bent on "making America"—whose presence and ambitions constituted a challenge to the Creoles. And they certainly had similar despairing sentiments about the seeming powerlessness of the motherland and its ruling Bourbon monarch Charles IV knuckling under to the French, who had broken the First Coalition against the revolution in 1795, compelling the Spanish to cede the eastern two-thirds of Hispaniola and to join them as allies in the European war. From that time France systematically reduced Spain to a military and economic satellite. There were other similarities between Venezuela and Buenos Aires, of course. Each would be the origin of a revolution and independence movement that would spread to the Pacific coast of Spanish South America. Each would elevate a military commander—Bolívar in the north, José de San Martín in the south—to command of armies of people of color. But each would produce a different kind of revolution and leader.

Some of the disaffected Creoles looked to the American Revolution for inspiration. Although they had little regard for the kind of society that had taken root in the young United States, they did admire the audacity and determination of its revolutionary generation in challenging the world's greatest power. Spanish Americans had their own "Jeffersonian" voice, Juan Pablo Viscardo y Guzmán, one of the Jesuits expelled by the Spanish crown during the "second conquest," the phrase modern historians use to describe the efforts of the Spanish Crown to reassert its authority over its American kingdoms in the late eighteenth century. Viscardo's fiery tract, "Open Letter to American Spaniards," advanced the case for the children of the conquerors to benefit from their valor and labor as eloquently as Jefferson's *Summary View of the Rights of British Americans*. The North American revolutionary experience, of course, had culminated in a postwar nation very different and more deeply fractured than that imagined by later generations, but its independence had not been reversed.[3]

Yet, even for the most outspoken among them, the most disturbing scenario lay in Haiti. In 1798, the British withdrew their troops and, following a struggle for power with the leader of colored forces, Toussaint-Louverture emerged triumphant and for a few years ruled Saint-Domingue as French governor-general of a de facto autonomous colony and maintained its plantation economy with a severe labor code. But the settlement of the undeclared war between France and the United States coupled with a truce in the fighting in Europe prompted Napoleon to reaffirm French control over the island and reintroduce slavery. That act precipitated two years of destructive and infuriatingly complex warfare. Although the fighting had largely ended with the establishment of the independent state in January 1804, Haiti embodied every social, economic, and political attribute white Creoles feared. The 1805 Haitian constitution officially abolished distinctions based on color and all forms of servitude. Its first governor-general, Jean-Jacques Dessalines, had doggedly tried to maintain the plantation economy by continuing the coercive labor policy Toussaint-Louverture had established, but what most Venezuelans (and North Americans) remembered about the man was his infamous decree ordering the execution of those French who had refused to leave the country for their centuries of barbaric treatment of the slaves. Venezuelan Creoles feared only too well that their slaves harbored similar vengeful sentiments.

The prospects for Venezuelans, then, were uncertain. They might emulate the porteño Creoles or take some satisfaction that their grievances were as justifiable as those expressed by British Americans in 1776, but Venezuela was like neither of these places. If they persisted, the calamity that might befall them would be far more disastrous.

The Rebellion

What prompted Venezuela's Creoles to renew their litany of complaints were accounts of Napoleon's efforts to incorporate a pliant Spanish royal house more fully into his continental economic system. In September 1807 Napoleon had issued an ultimatum to Portuguese Prince Regent João to choose joining either Britain or France in the war. When he vacillated, Napoleon dispatched an invading army, and in mid-November a British fleet arrived to transport the royal family to safety in Brazil. The Spanish royal family was not so fortunate. In March 1808 French troops began gathering in northern Spain. In this instance, Napoleon had an accomplice, Manuel Godoy, court intriguer and lover of Spanish queen María Luisa. In return for his services, Godoy wanted authority over southern Portugal. Napoleon issued Charles an ultimatum to surrender his kingdom. When rumors circulated that the royal family might try to flee, a mob surrounded the royal palace at Aranjuez and compelled the abdication of the king in favor of his popular son, Ferdinand. For a brief time, the new monarch enjoyed the acclaim befitting his title, the Desired One. With a French army to back him up, the father now asked for his throne back on the grounds he had abdicated under pressure. Napoleon proved too crafty to permit such a reversal. On the pretext of settling the issue, he lured both father and son to France, a journey culminating in their forced abdication and the naming of Joseph Bonaparte as king of Spain and his possessions in the Americas.

Throughout Spain there was resistance, organized initially by provincial juntas and then in a central junta in Seville, which on September 18 pronounced its fidelity to Ferdinand and, according to stories later circulating among Venezuelans, a Spanish national assembly "declared war" on France. A Spanish official in Caracas discounted that tale as a British fabrication.

Only when they learned that a Bonaparte ruled in Madrid and that Ferdinand was indeed a prisoner did the Creoles realize their future was uncertain. To whom should they pledge their loyalty? Their predicament was dissimilar to that of British Americans in 1776 or those Brazilians who had received a Portuguese monarch fleeing Napoleon's grasp in 1807. In the Spanish tradition, the people did not retain sovereignty but "alienated" that right to the king. If the king were powerless or a captive, then the people could rightfully but temporarily reclaim that sovereignty until the king or his rightful successor was restored to power. But what did tradition hold if the king abdicated his power?

Potentially more troublesome to the *mantuanos* of Caracas and the neighboring valleys were the social and racial dimensions about the definition of the people in these calculations, who in their mind mattered little in their long-standing demand for equality with Spaniards. For the time being, however, Creoles in Venezuela (and elsewhere in Spanish America) made their choice clear: Joseph Bonaparte was a usurper, and Ferdinand VII (the Desired One) the rightful claimant to the Spanish throne. When French emissaries visited Caracas in summer 1808, the protesting *caraqueños* plastered Ferdinand's portrait throughout the city. Contrastingly, representatives from the newly founded National Assembly arrived to celebratory welcomes and donations of jewelry and gold pesos to the cause of restoring Ferdinand to his throne.

Throughout Spanish America's provincial capitals, Venezuela's Creoles had kindred spirits. The Creoles shepherding these protests invoked an honored Spanish urban tradition by reviving a form of city government, the *cabildo abierto*. In virtually every place and except in all but the most radical among them, those dominating these cabildos wanted recognition of their place as equals within the Spanish "transatlantic family," not independence. On the surface, their demands bore a similarity to the moderate position of discontented British-American colonials at the First Continental Congress (September–October 1774) calling not for independence but for affirmation of their rights as Englishmen and the equivalence of autonomy. Protest movements against the arbitrariness of parliamentary legislation had erupted in the cities of the North Atlantic seaboard. Although in both cases the evidence is more intuitive than tangible, it can be argued that those Creoles demanding equality with Spaniards were, like their British-American counterparts, reaffirming historic rights and their membership as equals within the Spanish familial nation. Certainly, British, French, and even Spanish liberal thinking sustained the idea that a compatriot in America shared the same rights as one in the mother country.

For other equally compelling reasons, both the Spanish resistance to the French occupation and the Spanish-American cause during the critical two years from 1808 to 1810 bore little resemblance to what had occurred in the British Empire on the eve of the American Revolution. The motherland had been occupied by French troops. Ferdinand, the rightful monarch, was an exiled captive. There were *afrancesados* or "Frenchified" Spaniards and their patriot adversaries. In January 1809 the Central Junta of Spain (now located in Seville), created in his name, decreed the equality of Spanish-American dominions with those of the motherland and granted them representation. In January 1810 the Central Junta (reformed as a Supreme Council of Regency) was empowered to call a parliament (*cortes*) for writing a new constitution for Spain and America. In Caracas, the befuddled captain-general, Juan de Casas, wavered throughout these days between accepting the authority of the Central Junta and its successor and the monarch in whose name it professed to govern or acquiesce to the pressures from those calling for an autonomous junta. Ultimately, he bowed to the wishes of the demonstrators and called a meeting of Caracas's notables to discuss the situation.

For those who believed that reform was the best preventive of rebellion or revolution, such an approach should have placated the disaffected Creoles and even those Peninsulars upset over the French invasion. After all, those Spaniards united against the French usurpers had come a long way toward recognizing the legitimacy of their claims of equality with the declaration that Spanish America was neither colony nor plantation but an integral part of the Spanish monarchy and as recognition of its status had been granted representation in the *cortes*. Thus, for most Spaniards, whether residing in the peninsula or overseas, the legitimacy of the Spanish nation—what Bolívar in his famous 1815 Jamaica Letter called a "community of interests, of understanding, [and] of religion"—had apparently survived the political uncertainties created by the French invasion of the motherland and the Spanish uprising against it.[4]

Those were strong sentiments—just as compelling as the affection many English in the Atlantic colonies felt for the homeland on the eve of revolution—but, as in the British-American case, they were beliefs sorely tested by the times. The gathering of European and American Spaniards in one body served largely to bring out the fundamental divisions between the two—the former favoring acquiescence to the new political order; the latter calling for a local junta—but did not immediately produce a call for action. When Casas learned about the creation of provincial juntas in Spain, however, he suggested that Caracas's notables might wish to reconsider following their example. He soon regretted the decision. When Casas received the list of eighteen members of the proposed junta—whose membership reflected civil, clerical, military, university, legal, planter, and business interests as well as the people—he sensed that such a move would largely serve to encourage a republican conspiracy. The advocates of a junta persisted, and in late November 1808 they presented Casas with yet another petition. On this occasion, the captain-general mobilized a pardo militia and arrested the petitioners, some of whom remained under house confinement for six months.

Bolívar was not a party to this alleged conspiracy of mantuanos, as the petitioners were called. But he was not indifferent to the continually shifting political winds over the next two years. Off and on he met with other discontented Creoles and, on occasion, even spoke publicly about conditions in Venezuela. And, just as often, he was ever cautious and even conciliatory toward Spanish officials, among them the new captain-general, Vincente de Emparán, who arrived in May 1809. Emparan admired France and Napoleon but opposed the restrictive colonial trade laws and moved easily among the Creoles. Bolívar himself enjoyed his company. In different circumstances, perhaps, Emparán's lenient approach might have proved successful in placating the mantuano elites, but he could go only so far in accommodating their wishes. At bottom, as before, the question was one of loyalty. They could bow to the Council of Regency and dispatch delegates to the projected cortes or they could continue pressing for a local junta that persistently rejected the authority of the Regency, but such a choice struck Spanish authorities as tantamount to subversion.

In April 1810, Venezuela's Creole dissidents made their decision. They deposed Emparán and organized a governing junta in the name of Ferdinand. In the following months, other Spanish-American cities followed a similar pattern of action. In almost every case, their decision depended on local whims and circumstances, but virtually all those who joined these movements believed that they had no assurances the detested French would ever leave Spain, nor could they reconcile the professions of equal treatment for overseas Spain with the reality that they must acquiesce in the decisions made by the Regency. Beyond those certainties, the motives of those who rejoiced in the revival of the junta were both bewildering and ambiguous. They wished to be free of the control of the Regency yet retain all the trappings as well as the symbolism of monarchical rule.

Autonomy perhaps best described their agenda. The idea possessed undeniable appeal to those who believed that the political rights of overseas Spain could be reconciled with the spiritual belief in a unified Spanish nation, one and indivisible, where the distinctive regions were equal. For many transatlantic liberals who had watched the Atlantic world descend into rebellion and revolution, it was an idea whose time had come. In the mid-eighteenth century, Benjamin Franklin had written about prosperous British colonies assuming their rightful place as equals with England. His ideas fell victim to the rising resentments over London's more forceful policies toward its Atlantic colonies, which culminated in the war for independence. In Saint-Domingue, Toussaint-Louverture took command over a slave rebellion that had erupted in 1791 and seven years later appeared triumphant over his enemies, foreign and domestic. Throughout, he insisted that the only way to preserve French rule in what had been the richest and most productive sugar regime in the world was to end slavery and permit an autonomous colony that would revive the plantation economy and restore prosperity. For a few years he governed the French colony as virtual dictator, but he did not survive the wrath of the more imperious Napoleon, whose agents lured the "Black Napoleon" into a trap and sent him in chains to a French prison. The reality, frankly, lay in the fact that neither the British nor the French government had shown a willingness to concede autonomy as long as its leaders were persuaded they could stifle any protest or rebellion in their American domains and as long as they believed such a concession was a sign of weakness.[5]

To Bolívar, the April 1810 Creole overthrow of the governor-general constituted an intermediate step along the route toward independence. His reasoning derived not so much from a singular historical example or body of thought but an amalgam of beliefs both personal and intellectual—a cultivated anti-Spanish bias, a hostility toward monarchy that grew out of his grounding in Enlightenment thought and his experience with Freemasonry, or, just as likely, his realization that if Venezuela became an autonomous entity, his place in any government would be marginal. In any event, when he got word of what the junta had done, he raced into Caracas and offered his military services to the new government. Venezuela's self-declared magistrates were not ready to field a military force, but they needed foreign aid and did want to take advantage of Bolívar's European experiences and connections. When Bolívar agreed to fund his own travel expenses, they sent him to London to obtain whatever support he could muster from the British government. His companions were Luis López Méndez and Bolívar's former tutor, Andrés Bello, who joined the delegation as secretary. (Juan Vicente and another commissioner sailed for the United States, with every expectation that the young republic would favor their cause. That mission proved fruitless, and the two cut short their trip. On the return voyage, Juan Vicente perished in a shipwreck.)

The London Mission

Bolívar arrived in Portsmouth on July 10, toting ambiguous instructions and a plea for assistance from a government quite willing to serve as advisor and protector, bound by treaty to support the Spanish nation in the war against France, and Ferdinand as its rightful king. But the British were leery of committing themselves to a cause lacking broad support. In its appeal to London the Caracas junta reaffirmed its loyalty to Ferdinand, and the instructions stressed the point that Venezuela remained an "integral part of the Spanish empire" and pledged to assist in the common struggle against the French enemy—sentiments that mirrored the public statements of the Council of Regency. For the Venezuelan emissaries, the gravamen of the Regency's case was the insistence that they must accept its jurisdiction. The most troublesome part of the instruction, as the British secretary for foreign affairs (Richard Wellesley) alertly noted, lay in the Venezuelans' appeal for British assistance to meet the anticipated retaliation of the council and those provinces that recognized its authority.[6]

The problem that ensued was in some respects Bolívar's own doing. When the Venezuelans met with Wellesley—an informal gathering, as the group lacked diplomatic status—Bolivar dutifully handed over his credentials and the instructions in a sealed envelope. As Wellesley scanned the documents, Bolívar in his best French began to catalog the iniquities of Spanish rule in Venezuela and the justness of independence. The British minister offered no comment until Bolívar finished his litany of complaints. Only then did Wellesley matter-of-factly observe that the instructions contained not a word about independence. The impetuous Bolívar had not read his instructions.

Wellesley could not accept the notion that the Regency lacked legitimacy and thus could not be recognized by Venezuela. That would be the equivalent of a declaration of independence, and for Britain to acknowledge such a course at a time when it very much needed a Spanish ally in the war against France and was at loggerheads with the U.S. government about maritime and trade issues might prove disastrous. When he tried to placate the Venezuelans with a comment that the British government would use its influence to obtain a change in the representation to the proposed cortes, they refused to back down. In the final moments of this contretemps, Bello tried to soothe both sides with a statement reaffirming the integrity of overseas Spain and the motherland (which the British clearly supported) and expressing the rights of the Caracas junta to pledge its loyalty to Ferdinand but not accept the jurisdiction of the Regency.[7]

For Bello, these were not empty words. They reflected a fundamental difference with his former student over the meaning of the rebellion and the ultimate goal of the April 1810 declaration. Throughout, Bello insisted that the political sovereignty of the emerging countries in Spanish America must have a moral and intellectual foundation. Otherwise, he predicted, their influence would be of no greater consequence than that of African tribes or the tiny islands of the ocean. Bolívar shared these sentiments and enthusiastically endorsed the idea of bringing Joseph Lancaster to Caracas in the belief that his tutoring system—"each one teach one"—would prove useful in educating a generation of Venezuelan children and thus shield them from the insidious influence of clerical indoctrination. Indeed, Bolívar went further than Bello in proposing the education of women as fundamental for inculcating a republican spirit.

What made these two men different was Bello's conviction that reform of the Spanish empire offered a far more acceptable path than independence for addressing legitimate Creole concerns. Bello remembered that Simoncito had been a gifted student but lacked the will to concentrate, and he could be careless, as the embarrassing incident in the meeting with Wellesley demonstrated. Though Bello was less than two years senior to his former pupil, their way of thinking about the conflict within the Spanish empire and its resolution sharply diverged. To Bello, the idea of independence was tantamount to rejection of membership in the transatlantic Spanish family. For Bolívar, the dream of separation from a corrupted and defiled motherland was a matter of moral and indeed personal conviction.[8]

The failure to obtain London's blessing for the Venezuelan cause did not lessen Bolívar's admiration for everything British—its constitutional monarchy, its socially responsible and service elite that offered a marked contrast to Europe's decadent aristocracy, and especially its power. He had an expansive view of British society during his short-lived diplomatic assignment. The contrast with his memory of Spain and even France a few years earlier was striking. Spanish aristocrats were either corrupt or feeble; revolutionary France had devoured its royalists and, if he had paused to dwell on it, not a few of its revolutionaries. Britain was different. Its social elite prepared for the future. With the intercession of Miranda, he consulted with the utilitarian philosopher Jeremy Bentham, who was then crafting a constitutional code and a Law of the Liberty of the Press for Venezuela. He dined with the anti–slave trade publicist William Wilberforce. He chatted with influential editors of London's press and listened to the plans of the city's social reformers for prison reform and the amelioration of child labor conditions.

In brief, he was easily persuaded that British society and culture could serve as a model for the new Venezuela—a privileged but socially responsible elite, an educational system preparing successive generations for their role as citizens in the new civic culture, and, more than anything else, stable and strong leadership that ensured a progressive and prosperous future. But what did the hypothetical questions Bolívar asked in 1810 have to do with the readiness of Venezuela for such a society? Could British social and political institutions be adapted in a culture that in his estimation had been so ill prepared for modernity? He recalled a phrase from Socrates: however well made, the shoe does not fit every foot.

In one task, at least, he was successful. Over the objections of his colleagues, he persuaded Miranda to return to Venezuela with him. To the others, Miranda was too dangerous, and like Bolívar unwilling to admit that Venezuelan independence was a fantasy and certainly too risky. Neither the British nor the North Americans would come to their aid, at least not yet. But Bolívar would not be dissuaded, and over the next few weeks he cultivated the old warrior—his senior by more than three decades—who shared Bolívar's fascination with Freemasonry and Enlightenment thought and was by reputation his equal as a lover. Miranda had spent several years building a network of Spanish-American aficionados. His reputation as the spokesman of the Spanish-American cause in the citadel of the world's greatest power was assured. Despite mounting debts, he enjoyed a secure and apparently happy life. He was nearly sixty. And if he did not know, he certainly must have sensed that no one else in the delegation or in the Caracas junta wanted him back in Venezuela. But Bolívar appealed to his revolutionary vanity by telling him that his return was vital to the cause for which he had struggled for two decades.[9]

The Declaration of Independence

Bolívar departed England aboard one of His Majesty's warships in September 1810. As a declared enemy of Spain, Miranda was denied permission to accompany him and secretly left the country that had provided him sanctuary a few weeks later. López and Bello remained in London to continue efforts to obtain British support for the Venezuelan cause, however dim the prospects for obtaining it.

On his return Bolívar ruefully concluded that little had changed in his absence, at least in his estimation. But over the course of the preceding months, Venezuela's government defied the council in numerous ways. It proclaimed free trade with neutrals and friendly nations and reduced export duties to further commerce. It abolished the *alcabala*, a sales tax on commonly used articles, as well as the tribute imposed on Indians. In retaliation the council responded with a proclamation that Venezuelans no longer suffered from an oppressive government but were incorporated as equals in the Spanish nation. The Venezuelans did not back down. To punish them, the council declared a blockade of the Venezuelan coast. Bolívar had gotten news of the blockade while he was still in London, and he reacted by calling for a declaration of war against Spain. But which Spain? He had in mind the Council of Regency—a government he later called our "unnatural stepmother"—but that Spain now benefited from professions of support of three Venezuelan provinces (Coro, Maracaibo, and Guiana) apparently motivated less by loyalty to the council than by hatred for the Creole usurpers. In these provinces, news of the blockade had prompted the public to celebrate with torchlight parades and *Te Deum* chants in the churches. When the provincial defectors took up arms, the Caracas government had no choice but to respond, but in the aftermath of victory over the insurgents it purposefully avoided meting out severe punishments, a policy Bolívar interpreted as weakness, a sentiment shared by those castas and pardos who had joined these movements.

The violence and the response to it paled by comparison with events in Mexico in fall 1810. There, a Creole conspiracy to gain control of Spain's richest kingdom had unexpectedly precipitated a massive popular uprising under the command of a Creole priest, Miguel Hidalgo, in the Bajío region of northwest Mexico. Confronted with an army of 80,000—Indians, dispossessed tenants, unemployed miners, artisans, priests, bandits, among others— with no singularity of purpose save perhaps revenge against those who abused them, Creoles instinctively joined Peninsulars in crushing the movement. What occurred in Venezuela was a portent of a violent social upheaval, as the U.S. commercial agent opined in November, "with the design of seizing and usurping the Executive power, of massacreing all the Europeans, & lastly of freeing the negroes, and placing the mulattoes & them on an equal footing with the rest of the whites."[10]

For Bolívar, the fundamental issue lay in the failure of leadership in the Caracas government. Those at the bottom of the social ladder must be led, and the message they desperately wanted to hear, he naively believed, was independence. He welcomed Miranda's arrival and labored daily against those in power who noised about stories of Miranda as a British agent conspiring to seize power and turn over a Catholic people to a Protestant imperial ruler. Bolívar's propaganda campaign must have been effective, as fearful Creoles soon abandoned their efforts to prevent Miranda's landing. On December 12, to the ovations of a welcoming crowd, the old warrior disembarked at the Venezuelan port of La Guayra, wearing a 1793 French general's uniform—blue tunic, white trousers, black boots, and two-cornered hat.

From that moment the two commenced their personal campaign for independence. For their part, members of the government and most of the old Creole families dismissed Miranda as a troublemaker and merchant's son, but his reputation—a victim of the Inquisition, French revolutionary general, and confidant of a former British prime minister—bespoke a loftier status, and his former detractors elected to name him a lieutenant-general. Miranda affected a populist demeanor, and he treated the pardos with a respect they rarely received from any white Venezuelan. Against such a record, who dared to suggest that a forty-year absence from Venezuela and a series of military failures made him singularly unqualified for the task of leading a movement for independence?

Bolívar would not levy such a charge, at least not in the early months of 1811, when the conflicting agendas and emotions raging among Venezuela's Creoles appeared to be on a collision course. On one side stood those who urged caution, reaffirming their commitment to Ferdinand yet just as determined to assert their autonomy. In early March they adopted the name of

Council for the Preservation of the Rights of the American Federation of Venezuela and Don Ferdinand, which was soon shortened to the National Congress. In the rival camp were those who belonged to the Patriotic Society, which had been founded in August 1810 to study the agriculture and ranching economy but had rapidly become a forum calling for independence. Its makeup, like that of the National Congress, was largely aristocratic, but its meetings included women and a smattering of voices from Caracas's popular classes. After his arrival in Venezuela, Miranda soon worked his way up to the presidency of the Patriotic Society. But Bolívar emerged as the most passionate speaker at its meetings.

The society put enormous pressure on the National Congress. On the first anniversary of the April 1810 declaration, the *Patriot of Venezuela* (a local broadside) formally called for independence. Two months later, a beleaguered Congress relented to the groundswell of protest and on July 1 approved a declaration of rights. Two days later, it convened to discuss independence but took no action. That evening, at the meeting of the Patriotic Society, Bolívar delivered one of his memorable political speeches, a denial of the accusation that the society was undermining national unity with its criticism of the Congress. "What we desire is that the union be effective, so that it may give us life in the glorious struggle to achieve our freedom," Bolívar declared. The Congress persisted in debating issues already settled and called for further consideration of "grand enterprises," an allusion to the patriot clamor for a formal declaration of independence. The times called for action, not further debate. Doubts about independence were little more than the "sad consequences of our ancient fetters," three centuries of Spanish misrule. The Congress must heed the call for independence and "lay the cornerstone of South American liberty; if we hesitate we are lost." In the end, the Congress did hesitate but for only one day. On July 5, after a stormy debate and with one dissenting vote, it declared the independence of the American Federation of Venezuela. The delegates' choice was as much the result of intimidation as conviction. José Domingo Díaz, a royalist observer of these events, compared the decision and the festivities that followed as one of the most depressing experiences of his life, a day and night when "decent" people watched fearfully as bands of whites, blacks, mulattoes, Spaniards, and Americans roamed wildly in the streets.[11]

The First Republic

The new political order began not in hope but in uncertainty. Crowds celebrated deliriously by ripping up Spanish flags and defacing portraits of

Ferdinand. But such outbursts of enthusiasm had little intimidating effect on the rapidly developing counterrevolution that had months before begun to harass those governing the country. In June and early July 1811, patriot forces had repulsed two royalist assaults in Cumaná province. In northwest Caracas, a gaggle of royalist Canary Islanders mounted on mules and armed with blunderbusses and cutlasses threatened gawking bystanders, who responded by hurling rocks. Troops from nearby Fort San Carlos soon arrived to quell the disturbance and, in a retaliation that shocked even some of the more fervent patriots, shot sixteen of the royalists and placed their decapitated heads at several places on the city's outskirts. The incident was a portent of the civil war that would soon engulf the country.

In the aftermath of several of the earlier confrontations between patriot and royalist, Bolívar had chastised the Executive Council for its tolerance of royalist defiance and violence against the patriots. His solution was a draconian one: Expel all Spaniards from the republic. The suggestion merely confirmed in Miranda's mind (and in others' as well) that Bolívar was a hothead whose ambition and blind hatred of the Spanish would doom the patriot cause. Nonetheless, the new government began to respond more forcefully to threats against it. When the Executive Council grew impatient with the failure of the republic's military commander (the Marqués de Toro) to put down another royalist threat in Valencia province, it turned to Miranda to take charge of the patriot army. The old revolutionary agreed to do so on condition that Bolívar not participate in the campaign as an officer. Bolívar was too rash in his behavior, Miranda believed. Bolívar's anger when he heard the news prompted the council to overrule Miranda. In this first public confrontation between two allies, Bolívar had demonstrated that his pride, ambition, and passion for a cause were inextricably linked. Years later, Bolívar confided to Daniel O'Leary, his aide and custodian of his correspondence, that Miranda and his compatriots believed Bolívar was impetuous and that they "regarded his ideas as the ravings of a delirious mind."[12]

The affair deepened his wariness of Miranda. Of the two, Miranda may have been more calculating. He was certainly more attentive to the international context of this struggle, particularly the intermittent British efforts to negotiate a truce between the patriots and the Regency while advancing its own interests in Venezuela. And as the son of a Canary Islander and longtime émigré who felt more comfortable with British and French officers, Miranda aroused suspicions among Creole patriots. Bolívar's distrust of him can be attributed to ego, jealousy, and a marked difference in temperament, but the growing rift between the two men conveyed something more ominous, at least as far as Bolívar was concerned. Increasingly, Miranda's behavior indicated that his commitment to independence was qualified and subject to negotiation. Bolívar's was not.[13]

The crux of the matter may very well have been Bolívar's insistence on the expulsion of all Spaniards from Venezuela and Miranda's persuasive argument that their dominance in the country's commercial life made them crucial to sustaining a weakened economy. But that was only one fundamental difference between the old rebel and the young upstart. Miranda was jealous of this "dangerous" young man who was always an intrusive presence. After the crushing of the Valencia uprising, when Miranda had to admit Bolívar performed well in battle, he reluctantly acknowledged that he had erred in trying to keep Bolívar out of the fight. But they had quarreled again over how to punish the defeated foe. Miranda chose a lenient course, but Bolívar pushed for an even more punitive campaign into other provinces he suspected remained loyal to the Crown. When Miranda demurred, the fiery Bolívar thought him irresolute.

At least they agreed on the need for a stronger central government to bind the fractious seven states of the country together. But in the final draft of the December 1811 constitution, federalist sentiments dominated. The document reflected some French and North American influences but largely followed the confederated pattern of Spanish American political organization. To the dismay of both Miranda and Bolívar, the new law virtually emasculated the central authority by delegating executive power to a committee of three men and permitting each state what amounted to self-rule. Miranda was quick to warn that such an arrangement would inevitably further divide Venezuelans, who were already quarreling over the rising tide of governmental expenditures.

Of the two, Bolívar was more outspoken about the defects of the new political order and especially the tolerance of its leaders toward those who deviated from its strictures. In reality, the explanation for the collapse of the first Venezuelan republic depended on both human and natural forces. In the beginning, the patriots possessed both inspiration and money, but over the course of a year they exhausted most of the three-million-peso booty they appropriated from the royal treasury on pensions, celebrations, salaries, and unusually high outlays for the military. In desperation, the government halved the wages of employees and commenced to issue paper money. As the economic crisis deepened, the country suffered another calamity. On March 26, 1812 (Maundy Thursday), an earthquake devastated Caracas, La Guaira, San Felipe, Barquisimeto, and Mérida, each of which had proclaimed independence. The royalist towns of Coro, Maracaibo, Valencia, and Angostura (modern Ciudad Bolívar) suffered virtually no damage. In the melee of terrified crowds and collapsing buildings of Caracas, where ten thousand perished, royalist priests told the shocked and wounded that the upheaval was God's punishment for their betrayal of the king and the true faith.

The republic never recovered from the disaster. According to a legendary tale, Bolívar acquitted himself well during the crisis. At what had been the San Jacinto convent, so the story goes, a deranged monk cried out for vengeance against a hapless patriot surrounded by an unruly throng. As the crowd moved menacingly toward the man, Bolívar miraculously emerged with his sword aloft and with a single blow felled the robed messenger of doom. "If nature is against us, we will fight her too, and make her do what we want," Bolívar proclaimed. A royalist who heard his boast described them as profane, but both the incident and Bolívar's outcry became a part of Venezuelan folklore.[14]

In the aftermath, the royalists mounted a counterattack from the west under the command of Domingo de Monteverde. A more immediate menace to the republic were the bands of roaming *llaneros*, brave and ferocious horsemen who had pledged their loyalty to the king and considered the declaration of independence little more than a Creole plot to exploit them. For the plainsmen, the Venezuelan war represented a tribal conflict between black and brown plainsmen who savored the freedom to live by their wits versus white Creoles determined to bring them under control. Their chief was a green-eyed, red-bearded Asturian, José Tomás Boves, a man of legendary bravery and rapacity who took pleasure in firing gunpowder in the faces of terrified captives before decapitating them or sticking banderillas in the necks of Creole dandies and compelling them to mimic a bullfight. He rewarded his bravest officers with gifts of the young ladies from the finest Creole families. Flaunting a skull flag on a black background, Boves mobilized ten thousand mounted warriors who fired plantations and slit masters' throats in the name of God and king. "Human dignity suffered outrages which even the Spaniards denounced with surprise and shame," Mijares wrote, implying that the Spaniards and not Bolívar began the infamous "war to the death."[15]

Boves embodied the defiance and independent spirit of the Venezuelan llaneros. Jailed by the first junta, he obtained his release with the friendly intervention of a Spanish official who correctly sensed that the llaneros were willing to carry out a racial war against whites, and that Boves would lead them. Among other things, they were incensed by the 1811 law code, which imposed the death penalty for the killing of cattle on the large ranches. Among his men, it was commonly understood that leniency was the mark of a coward. During one of the campaigns of early 1814, when exhausted Creoles and royalists called a momentary cessation of the fighting, Boves intentionally defied the order by unleashing a band of liberated slaves against the townspeople of Ocumare. According to stories of terrified survivors, the invaders raped women, killed indiscriminately, and in their rage severed ears, noses, breasts, and penises from corpses. When Bolívar learned of the atrocities, he ordered the execution of a thousand Spanish prisoners.[16]

Five years later, Bolívar would build a liberating army with these Venezuelan plainsmen. But in the somber days of spring 1812 neither he nor Miranda and certainly not the hapless triad of executives of the republic could have anticipated that the future of independent Venezuela lay with these people. Miranda had anticipated that the Spanish would take advantage of the chaos and emotional shock that came in the wake of the earthquake, and he had obtained from a reluctant Congress virtual dictatorial powers to preserve the independence of Venezuela. He decreed martial law, and in the face of growing public hostility began organizing an army for the defense of the country. He angered Creole plantation owners when he promised freedom to those slaves who would fight in the patriot cause for a decade. Slave owners were offered compensation, but they were more concerned about the loss of plantation labor and fears that the decision would incite mass killings of whites. Throughout Patriot ranks, his reputation diminished and, as they had done after the abortive invasions of 1806–1807, Venezuelans denounced him.

As he had done in the early months of the republic, Miranda relegated Bolívar to an assignment Simón believed was less befitting his talents—the defense of the republic's most important seacoast town, Puerto Cabello. Bolívar would surely have proved more resourceful than the overly cautious Miranda, who so doubted the capabilities of his troops that he hesitated before moving against Monteverde, who commanded a smaller force. As Bolívar anticipated, the morale among republic troops plummeted. His position in Puerto Cabello proved even more precarious. He had too few troops and little ammunition. The town's most important fort housed a number of wealthy political prisoners as well as vital supplies and munitions. In late June, the situation worsened when a group of rebellious soldiers seized the fort and turned its artillery against the town. Bolívar sent a desperate plea to Miranda for aid, noting that a Venezuelan officer had betrayed the cause, but when Miranda got the news he sensed it was too late to respond. In a poetic admission of hopelessness, he told his staff, "Venezuela is wounded in the heart. . . . That is the way of the world."[17]

On July 6, 1812, one year after the proclamation of Venezuelan independence, the exhausted republican garrison at Puerto Cabello surrendered. Bolívar and seven of his officers narrowly escaped arrest by fleeing to La Guaira. It was his first defeat, and he was humiliated. He provided Miranda with a plaintive explanation for the surrender and as punishment requested a reduction in rank. The old commander was already resigned to his own failure and the inevitable collapse of the republic. From the west, Monteverde's soldiers, reinforced by llanero bands, advanced toward Caracas. In the east, provinces that had once supplied the city with vital supplies fell under royalist control or collapsed into anarchy. In the end, as he had done in 1806, Miranda chose to abandon the cause. On July 12, he announced to his war council that he had signed an armistice.

Two weeks later, he departed for La Guaira where a ship waited to take him home to England. His intention may have been to obtain British assistance in order to renew the struggle, but, frankly, few Venezuelan patriots and certainly not Bolívar would have believed him. He was again denounced as he had been after the disastrous escapades of 1806 and 1807. On those occasions, at least, he had managed to avoid capture. This time he failed, and it was largely his own doing. When he arrived at the port, he foolishly ignored pleas from the captain to board ship and instead agreed to meet with a group of patriot officers. They demanded more details about his surrender. After he had taken leave of the group, they discussed what to do. Bolívar, in a decision he never repented, held out for executing Miranda as a traitor. But his fellow officers elected to surrender him to the Spanish.

In triumph Monteverde proved both vengeful and tolerant. He condemned the discredited Miranda to the fortress of La Guaira, where he lingered for two years. (Afterward, the precursor of Venezuelan independence was shipped to Spain, where he rotted away in the Prison of the Four Towers in Cádiz. He died on July 16, 1816, aged sixty-six.) In defiance of the surrender agreement he had signed with Miranda, Monteverde unleashed a campaign of persecution and terror against the patriot command. In a few instances, he exhibited an uncharacteristic humaneness toward his vanquished foes. One of the beneficiaries was Bolívar, who had slipped out of Puerto Cabello in disguise and taken refuge in the house of a friend in Caracas. But he could not hide out forever. Nor did he wish to suffer the fate of his comrades and spend the rest of his life in a Spanish prison. So he chose a third path: he appealed to a Basque friend, Francisco Iturbe, to speak for him. Iturbe led Bolívar before the newly appointed Governor Monteverde, offering his property as bond for the former commander of Puerto Cabello and winning the Spaniard over with a reminder that Bolívar had arrested Miranda. For that service to the king, Monteverde said, Bolívar would be permitted to leave Venezuela. Other Venezuelans who were present recalled that he had accepted the document saving him from prison with a defiant boast: "I arrested Miranda to punish a traitor, not to serve the king!" The outburst typified

Bolívar's rebelliousness, and at that moment he risked losing his passport to safety. Again, the persuasive Iturbe mollified the Spaniard. Monteverde permitted the rebel to escape. Only when Bolívar was out of his reach did he grasp his error. He had underestimated the resolve of this twenty-nine-year-old Venezuelan Creole. For months on end, it was said, the mention of Bolívar's name made Monteverde's face suddenly blanch.[18]

Was Bolívar grateful for what amounted to a pardon or repentant for taking up arms against the king or for what some would condemn as his betrayal of Miranda? Never. There were persistent rumors that he had turned Miranda over to the Spanish in order to save his own skin and protect his property from seizure, but those were conjectures that might have been believable for others who bargained their way out of Spanish jails but ill fit Bolívar's case. Bolívar was an opportunist, but he was not the sort who defied the established order in order to cut a deal. Nor was he the type of rebel who suffers a defeat and decides the cause really isn't worth another try. True, his initial behavior after getting his passport bespoke that of somebody who intended to take up a different life. Dining with a few friends, he talked about going to England and joining the army, but the comments proved to be little more than Bolivarian gab. His conversation was the kind of talk that came from someone both ambitious and passionate and whose every move and word conveyed an iron-willed determination about the rectitude of the cause he professed and a parallel uncertainty where that cause would lead.

Uncertainty was an apt description of the times, both in Spanish America and in Spain. In 1810, when the Spanish junta loyal to Ferdinand fled to Cádiz, Spanish liberals vowed to transform Spain into a constitutional monarchy. When they learned of the uprisings in Spanish America, their initial impulse called for suppressing them, but in 1808 there were fewer than 126,000 regular Spanish troops in America. More would be sent in the ensuing years, of course, but from the outset the resolution of Spanish commanders and especially ordinary soldiers to wage a long war to preserve the loyalty of overseas Spain remained in doubt. Venezuela was not yet a nation, but neither was Spain.

A time of uncertainty can also be a time of opportunity, and Bolívar had an intellectual and emotional makeup that called for continuing the fight. Monteverde had made a mistake. He had chosen the wrong person to forgive. He had let Bolívar go, and in that gesture of tolerance—what Bolívar later called an "act of stupidity"—he had unleashed the tiger. Bolívar resolved to make him pay for it by raising another army to restore Venezuela's honor. That quest would transform him into a revolutionary.

CHAPTER THREE

~

The Revolutionary

The collapse of the first Venezuelan republic was an ignominious end to an ambitious campaign, but the defeat did little to weaken Bolívar's resolve to renew the war. If anything, the short-lived experience of independence had renewed the determination of Venezuela's fractured and alienated movements—royalists, Creoles, pardos, blacks, and slaves—to stake their claim for control of the province. But if there were lessons to be learned from one year's experience, they were never easy to decipher, not even by those calculating Creoles or royalists who persisted in believing that they and not the mass of Venezuela's castas would be able to chart the province's future. Instinctively, each knew that perhaps the only means of winning the struggle lay in arming them yet feared what such a choice could mean. It was not a question of the paucity of ideas or models of governance. The Spanish tradition, and more recently the Constitution of 1812, offered a powerful example of inclusivity and resolution of conflict in a world swept by revolutionary fervor. That document constituted a triumphant achievement for transatlantic liberals, a charter committed to uniting the peoples of the Spanish world. Although those of African heritage did not enjoy full acceptance into the proposed new social order, by comparison with the other European empires in the Americas and even the United States, the 1812 Spanish constitution went much further in the granting of political privileges to and social acceptance of Indians and mestizos in overseas Spain.

The problem lay in too many ideas and especially too many examples—particularly the Haitian experience—in a society riven not only by localism but also by class and especially by color. At the time, Bolívar did not believe—indeed, he dared not let himself believe—that if he persisted, he and his Creole allies would be swallowed up by the forces they were unleashing. What mattered to Bolívar was his seemingly unshakable belief that Miranda and not he had betrayed the cause of independence, a judgment that others—among them his former tutor, Andrés Bello—would never accept. In their minds, Miranda the precursor of independence had recognized that the combinations of Monteverde's assault, the earthquake, the paucity of provisions, and the black uprising had constituted too formidable an obstacle to continuing the struggle. Clearly, Miranda lacked Bolívar's resolve, but neither did he possess the latter's royalist connections, and for this he paid the ultimate price—four years in a Cádiz prison and a death largely unmourned. For a decade, the unforgiving Bolívar denounced him as a coward and the betrayer of Venezuelan independence. Not until the patriot cause had triumphed did he acknowledge Miranda as an illustrious and even heroic figure in the struggle.

The Cartagena Manifesto

In any event, in late summer 1812, Bolívar had more immediate concerns. On September 1, he arrived in Dutch Curaçao, virtually penniless and facing further charges for the cost of the ship dispatched to Puerto Cabello to rescue him. By his own reckoning, he was treated rather shabbily, but by any objective assessment he was lucky to have escaped the punishment the Spanish meted out to Miranda. Dutch authorities confiscated his baggage, and for almost two months he survived on the charity of friends. He departed for rebellious Cartagena, New Granada, in late October, empowered with a 1,000-peso loan and the determination that he could persuade New Granadans that the recovery of Venezuela from the royalist grip must be their cause as well.

A more prudent observer would have described this as fanciful thinking on his part. When he landed in Cartagena, New Granada was riven with provincial and ideological feuds, and its most populous and richest province, Cundinamarca, was at the center of the storm. Created in March 1811 by an assembly pledging its loyalty to the deposed Ferdinand, Cundinamarca's first government reflected a strong federalist bias—a weak executive triumvirate and a strong legislature. In the chaotic months following the creation of local juntas, New Granadans sought to create a federation of equal and autonomous provinces with a weak central authority at the top. When that structure was formally crafted in late November 1811, then, the character of New

Granadan federalism more closely resembled the Articles of Confederation government in the United States, not the federalist artifice that replaced it under the 1787 Constitution.

This feeble effort to forge a spirit of unity among the provinces began to unravel almost from the onset. Although federalists prevailed in the Cundinamarca legislative body, its second president, Antonio Nariño, possessed centralist convictions and behaved accordingly. Nariño had suffered Spanish punishment in the 1790s for disseminating copies of the French Declaration of the Rights of Man. His successor, Camilo Torres, who had authored the defiant *Memorial de Agravios* (Petition of Grievances), initially professed federalist views, but he ultimately came around to Bolívar's way of thinking about the imperative of a strong central authority. Their differences, however, paled before the ideological and social feuds that effectively splintered New Granada into three blocs—royalist provinces, Cundinamarca, and the United Provinces. To make matters worse, when the Council of Regency insisted the province of Cartagena de las Indias accept its authority, radical leaders aroused the colored castes and compelled the local junta to acquiesce in their demand that Cartagena was a sovereign and independent entity.

When Bolívar docked in Cartagena, then, he encountered a civil war that in its provincial antagonisms appeared to resemble what he had fled in neighboring Venezuela, and in his determination to mobilize another invasion force he glossed over the differences. New Granada was more traditional and more Catholic, and, perhaps most critically, its racial configuration and dynamics were different. In 1800, Venezuelan whites numbered 185,000, approximately twenty percent of a population of 900,000. New Granada's white population, according to the royal census of 1778, stood at 215,000 (approximately twenty-six percent of a population of 827,000), but the critical difference between the two countries lay in Venezuela's larger numbers of slaves (111,000 and 66,000, respectively) and, especially, the more prevalent fear of slave uprising among Venezuelan Creoles. New Granada's incipient revolt of the late eighteenth century was the Comunero rebellion of 1781–1782, a protest against higher taxes imposed by imperial administrative demands. Although there were muted calls for independence and denunciations of "bad government," the racial dynamics of the affair bore little resemblance to what occurred in Venezuela in the Coro rebellion.[1]

At the time, understandably, this difference appeared less critical to Bolívar than other, more immediate issues. He had taken his cause to a people wary of both the man and his call for unity in a common cause. There was nothing comparable among New Granadans in their feelings about Caracas in 1812 to the rage expressed by British American colonials in 1775 over

London's punishment of Boston for its defiance of Parliament, yet in these troublesome months of late 1812, as the provinces of New Granada warred among themselves, Bolívar steeled himself to what was in fact a monumental task. He had to persuade New Granadans to join him in the liberation of Venezuela. In his appeal he sounded less like the exile with a catalog of grievances about the suffering of his homeland and more like the revolutionary espousing two universal principles: the need for unity among the provinces and the imperative of offensive warfare.

In mid-December 1812 Bolívar laid out his strategy in the first of his major political statements—an appeal to New Granadans to support the cause of their comrades in Venezuela and, more important, to avoid the errors committed by the Caracas junta during the stormy days of the first republic. The Cartagena Manifesto read like a damning collective indictment of errors committed by Venezuela's first generation of rulers—the "fatal adoption of the governing ideal of tolerance" or, more damnable, the governing junta's restraint in "liberating by force any town too stupid to see the value of its rights." Obsessed with the ideal of political perfection and unmindful of the need for practical governance, independent Venezuela had permitted Spaniards to remain in the country and, when they had engaged in conspiracies against the state, had hesitated to mete out punishment. The juntas had preferred poorly trained militias over veteran troops to safeguard independence—a complaint George Washington often voiced—and the consequence was clear: "We ended up with philosophers for generals, philanthropy for legislation, dialectics for tactics, and sophists for soldiers."[2]

He reserved his most stinging words for attributing the collapse of the "stupid republic" to the junta's decision to adopt a federalist system and its exaggerated faith in the rights of man. Here, Bolívar's reasoning conformed to his habit of invoking inspirational political and social ideas only to point out their inappropriateness for Venezuelans and, by implication, other rebellious Spanish Americans and, presumably, his North American contemporaries. Federalism was indeed "the most perfect and suitable for guaranteeing human happiness in society," he conceded, but it was a "form [of government] most inimical to the interests of our emerging states [because] . . . our fellow citizens are not yet ready to take on the full and independent exercise of their rights, because they lack the political virtues marking the true citizen of a republic."[3]

Modern and contemporary analysts of Bolivarian statements have often pointed to the Cartagena Manifesto, as the *Memorial* is generally known, as perhaps the first indicator of a temperament too accepting of strong executive power and even dictatorship, thus laying the foundation for his severe rule during the short-lived second Venezuelan republic and, by implication, his hostility toward federalism and seemingly instinctive pessimism about democracy. Others, more attuned to the undeniable prevalence of gendered language in revolutionary discourse, have framed the Cartagena Manifesto as Bolívar's invocation of a "masculine" obligation to impose the rule of order over a naive generation endangered because of its "feminine" tolerance and respect for self-determination and human rights. Perhaps the first republic had deserved its fate, but in his mind it also warranted rescue. More important, as long as he persisted in believing that there was no alternative to independence, his task remained one of forging a unified force and proclaiming the bonds between two peoples: "Do not be deaf to the pleas of our brothers. Rush forth to avenge death, to give life to the dying, succor to the oppressed, and freedom to all."[4]

The Admirable Campaign

Bolívar had yet to prove the worthiness of this cause to his newfound benefactors. He began by undertaking a daring assault on royalist towns along the Magdalena River. The campaign was an example of Bolívar's style of offensive warfare and, frankly, disobedience of instructions to maintain a strictly defensive posture. His audacity and bravura raised republican spirits. There followed an even more critical victory over Spanish troops at Cúcuta, which lay on the border with Venezuela and which offered Bolívar a base from which to launch the invasion of his homeland. In a relatively brief period, his military prowess and daring had impressed his superiors. The government of the United Provinces named him brigadier general and authorized him to invade Venezuela with an army made up largely of New Granadan troops. But he was to progress no farther than Trujillo and, more troubling to Bolívar, he must restore the federalist regime he had so thoroughly savaged in the Cartagena Manifesto.

By early March the invaders had reached the Venezuelan town of San Antonio, where Bolívar invoked a biblical analogy in proclaiming to his soldiers that the crusade for the liberation of Venezuela had commenced. Already, political squabbling among his fellow officers over his commitment to liberating Venezuela had caused problems for him. Bolívar had yet to fashion a loyal cadre nor had he persuaded his civilian superiors in the New Granadan congress of the urgency of his mission. He had yet to frame his war strategy in continental terms. His war remained a personal struggle, but in these early days of the "Admirable Campaign" to liberate Venezuela, his determination once again paid off. One of his rivals, Colonel Manuel

Castillo, embittered over Bolívar's appointment as brigadier general, re-signed, which in turn precipitated even more grumbling in the ranks and numerous desertions. Castillo's replacement and ally, the handsome Major Francisco de Paula Santander, proved so obstreperous in taking orders that in an angry retort Bolívar threatened to shoot him.

The affair did not resolve what ultimately proved to be fundamental differences between Bolívar and his New Granadan allies, but in his as-sertiveness Bolívar again displayed those qualities that marked him as a leader, albeit one who could be demanding of his subordinates. The rift with Santander, who would become his vice president with the 1819 union of Venezuela, New Granada, and Quito into Gran Colombia, would fester for years. Such conflicts have multiple explanations—Bolívar's ambition, jealousies of his comrades, Bolívar's seemingly instinctive habit of demand-ing deference, and so on. But the most plausible, I believe, was his desper-ate need for reassurance from those closest to him that he played not only an important but an essential role in the patriot cause. That was Bolívar's definition of loyalty—unquestioning and personal commitment. Another Venezuelan, Colonel Rafael Urdaneta, grasped what Bolívar was seeking when he promised: "General, if two men are enough to free the country, I am ready to go with you."[5]

Bolívar needed such a commitment and more. His forces were still out-numbered, but he now enjoyed an unanticipated advantage—the inexpli-cable cruelty of Monteverde's counterrevolution in Venezuela, an ordeal of terror and barbarism, which to Bolívar justified equally harsh responses, up to a point. One Venezuelan patriot, Antonio Briceño ("The Devil"), reput-edly had promised to reward his followers if they brought him the head of a Spanish enemy. Not even the vengeful Bolívar resorted to such excesses. But the savagery of the Venezuelan civil war did prompt him to issue his most controversial proclamation, "War to the Death," on June 15, 1813, a pardon to Spaniards and Canary Islanders who joined the patriot cause, forgiveness and immunity to Americans regardless of their crimes against the struggle, and death to Spaniards and Canary Islanders who professed neutrality.[6]

The decree was his first serious effort to define a nation and to create a loyal following for what he saw as a rejuvenation of the independence move-ment. Spanish miscalculation abetted his cause. Monteverde had intention-ally tarried in proclaiming the liberal constitution until November 1812 and, in effect, had imposed the harshest regimen against defiant Venezuelan Creoles. Neither had the royalist commander satisfied the growing demands of pardos and slaves, most of whom had joined the counterrevolution, for equality. The War to the Death decree, Bolívar reckoned, should compel those trying to survive in the chaotic environment of the civil war to make a choice. He had not yet taken a precise measure of the narrow social base of the independence movement. He had not yet fully assessed the degree of psychological damage the War to the Death decree might do to the reputation of the patriot cause in Europe and the United States.

In any event, a string of victories in summer 1813 coupled with royalist disarray enabled Bolívar (who now held the title of Liberator) to enter his beloved Caracas in triumph on August 7, 1813. The victory represented a personal triumph. What followed was the first of numerous festive celebrations. Bolívar relished the occasion. To the cries of "Viva el Libertador de Venezuela," he moved through a crowd of well-wishers and supporters. In the evening he attended a ball given in his honor and from that moment commenced a four-year affair with an adoring twenty-year-old, Josefina Machado. But the most telling consequence of these early days of the second republic was Bolívar's explanation to the Supreme Congress of New Granada that in order to deal with the anarchy plaguing the city, he intended to exercise supreme authority.[7]

A Dictatorship of Necessity

Bolívar was the city's savior and its despot. He gloried in the former and stubbornly insisted that only a forceful executive would enable Venezuela to sustain the republic. He could not be a monarch, and he would not be a federalist functionary. "Republican monarch" (a term aptly describing George Washington) would have been an equally suitable title for Bolívar's way of thinking about executive power. When he got word that the new governor of Barinas province was calling for the restoration of the federalist constitution, he dictated a letter reminding the governor that England and France held sway in the world because their central governments were powerful. Anticipating that the governor would cite the example of the United States as a respected federalist government, Bolívar pointed out that its first central government had been recognized by its former enemy and that its states, though sovereign, did not exercise authority over the treasury, war, or foreign relations. In New Granada, contrastingly, the demands for provincial autonomy and separation of powers had precipitated civil war. "I have not liberated Venezuela," he wrote in defiant tones, "to install the same system."[8]

In the meantime, he confronted other problems. Inevitably, the War to the Death decree prompted criticism and outcries, and not only from royalist apologists. Several of his putative allies in New Granada had already begun to question his military strategy. One of his accusers, the brigadier Joaquín Ricaurte, denounced the War to the Death decree as a "barbarous and impolitic project" that would do irreparable damage to the patriot cause. Probably, but the decision had all the marking of political expediency and what O'Leary called the "stamp of frankness" and "dire necessity." Bolívar had used words similar to those in the *Law of Suspects* issued in revolutionary France in 1793, which condemned to death those who had "done nothing" for liberty. The French might die for such abstractions or condemn to death those who would not, but what did that have to do with Venezuela? What mattered was Bolívar's intention in issuing the decree. He meant it as a threat to be enforced in extreme circumstances, and he ordered its suspension in the belief that Monteverde might accept his offer of reconciliation and the opportunity for disaffected Spaniards to emigrate. Spaniards had commenced the war to the death. They treated Americans as traitors and not belligerents worthy of equal treatment, and they would never give up without such harsh measures. And there was more. The world must recognize the worthiness of the Spanish-American cause. The War to the Death decree, Mijares has noted, served as a reminder of "severe punishment" to a people with a "sense of impunity . . . that justice, tolerance and compassion could be demanded as rules for public life on this side of the Atlantic, too."[9]

The decree represented as well Bolívar's efforts to define the Venezuelan nation, not by color or ethnicity but by place and especially commitment to a cause. But who were Venezuelans? And what was their cause? Though doubtless there were signs that patriot propaganda had filtered down into the social order, Bolívar had not emerged as the voice of those from below. He was not one of them. Nor was he their leader. Nonetheless, in September 1813 he chose to proclaim the goals of the independence movement in a manifesto to the world, a catalog of royalist atrocities in Venezuela and an impassioned appeal to the nations of the world for understanding of the justice of the patriot cause. Monteverde had invaded Venezuela in defiance of orders, Bolívar insisted. He had permitted Boves and his gangs of llanero bandits to terrorize a hapless population and incited a slave and pardo revolt in the eastern valleys and seacoast—all in a defiant mockery of the 1812 constitution. In the final passage he again demonstrated that he was fighting a personal war. "I shall fight," he wrote, "until I eradicate every last Spaniard from the provinces of Venezuela that have experienced the excess of their tyranny, their injustice, their perfidy, and their atrocities . . . or I will die in the effort."[10] His words bespoke commitment and passion. They conveyed also defiance and a parallel determination to continue the struggle whatever the cost.

Circumstances did not favor the patriot cause. In October 1813, as Bolívar penned yet another of his letters demonizing Spanish royalists for their barbarous rule of Venezuela to the British governor of Curaçao, the first session of the Spanish Cortes created by the 1812 constitution convened in Cádiz. Though not represented in numbers proportional to its population (16 million to 10.5 million for Spain), the reality that Spanish America had at long last achieved a constitutional legitimacy within the Spanish nation provided reassurance to those who believed in home rule. Royal authority had eroded. Over the next five months virtually all Spain was liberated from French rule. The long muted cause of Spanish liberalism had triumphed—at least for the moment.[11]

If anything, these events in the homeland could only weaken patriot resolve and the support for independence. In fall 1813, Bolívar confronted more immediate challenges. He had won the battle for Caracas, but he did not rule all Venezuela. Royalist troops remained in Maracaibo, Coro, and Guayana. His old nemesis Monteverde, emboldened by the arrival of fresh troops, defiantly spurned offers of surrender. And within the patriot armies there were dissident voices. General Santiago Mariño, whose forces had liberated the eastern provinces of Cumaná and Barcelona, persistently refused to acknowledge Bolívar as his military commander. Worse, the government was soon mired in an economic crisis brought on by the expenses of fighting a civil war and the predictable resistance of agricultural producers to forced loans. Ominously, by the end of the year it was clear that patriot overtures and especially government policies had accomplished little to diminish pardo resentments over Creole rule and, if anything, had deepened suspicions about the promise of independence. Popular participation in the independence movement had been as strong in Venezuela as in any other region of Spanish America—save, perhaps, for Mexico—but the patriot cause had benefited less, as the rebellious slaves and pardos joined royalist guerrilla bands who took out their racial hatreds against white Creole property owners.

In early 1814, as Bolívar speculated about how the rapidly changing military situation in both Europe and North America would impact on the patriot cause, Venezuela collapsed into a sanguinary racial and class war. Boves and his "Legion of Hell" recaptured the plains, where the government's restrictions on hunting and travel had roused the fiercely independent llaneros. Here the war was neither about monarchical absolutism or republican ideals. Bolívar paid his troops with grants of property. Boves rewarded his followers by permitting them to pillage and to divide among themselves the property of their victims. In these circumstances, Bolívar's efforts to placate the royalists by extending pardons and amnesties to those who had taken up arms against the republic had little impact on mitigating the conflict. Shortly, he resumed the execution of Spaniards. When the archbishop of Venezuela expressed concern about the severity of his policies, Bolívar explained that Boves had killed "without distinction," thus justifying the "severe measures . . . [to] avenge my country and to curb the rage of its destroyers."[12]

In spring and summer 1814 royalist forces and the scattering of guerrilla bands swept across the Venezuelan countryside, leaving in their wake tales of death and destruction that reminded chroniclers of the most frightening excesses of the Haitian revolution. By early July Bolívar resolved to abandon Caracas. He took with him the remnants of a demoralized army, 20,000 men, women, and children, and twenty-four boxes filled with silver and jewelry from the city's churches. In the confusion and hysteria that engulfed Caracas, he quickly came under suspicion as a thief and a deserter. His principal accusers were José Félix Ribas, who had assumed command of the skeletal patriot army, and its highest ranking pardo officer, Manuel Piar. When Bolívar got wind of the charges, he elected to return the moneys, jewelry, and munitions as a sign of his good intentions. Ribas was unmoved by the gesture and ordered him arrested. In these circumstances, Bolívar might very well have suffered the same fate as Miranda, but for the second time in as many years he obtained his release, this time by persuading his guards that he was innocent. By the time Ribas learned about what had happened, Bolívar was on his way out of the country.

Ribas may have had understandable questions about Bolívar's motives for leaving Caracas and taking so much of its transportable wealth with him. Piar harbored doubts about Bolívar as well. As a pardo himself, Piar became increasingly alert to the racial dimensions of the war, the gnawing doubts among the pardos about their place in a republican social order, and his relationship with the pardo troops. Ideas such as freedom, liberty, self-determination, and individual identity resonated differently in the minds of people of color. By drawing a line between American and Spaniard in the War to the Death decree, Bolívar had addressed the issue of the place of one's parentage in determining who would be spared, but he had not dared to tackle the far more explosive social question about color.

In a monarchical society, such matters were more easily resolved than in a republican social order, which explains in part why in the American Revolution the majority of indigenous peoples and African-American slaves perceived a less promising future in the new republican order than they had experienced under a British sovereign. Bolívar had already accepted pardos into the patriot ranks because the royalists had done so. Within two years, he would go further by advocating the arming of slaves, which his Creole associates found even more unsettling and economically damaging because the practice deprived them of a labor force. But there were limits to how far a military leader could blur the color line. Old doubts about the narrow social base of the independence movement might be mitigated by the acceptance of people of color in the patriot army but they were not likely to be obliterated, even in victory. And what neutral observer would indict people of color for subordinating nation to race in a society where nation was subordinated to rank and privilege?

For the moment, Bolívar had no time to dwell on these matters. In flight and under fire for deserting the cause he had so passionately vowed to defend, he issued a manifesto to the Venezuelan people explaining why he had abandoned Caracas. The tone of the document was both fatalistic and inspirational. If victory had eluded the patriots, the fault lay in the "inconceivable madness on the part of the American peoples which forced them to take up arms to destroy their liberators and restore the scepter to their tyrants." In the Cartagena Manifesto he had indicted the federalist system of government for the ills befalling the first republic. Neither "ineptitude nor cowardice" explained the collapse of the second so much as the enormity of establishing "liberty in a country of slaves" in such a brief time. He grieved over his own role in the nation's calamity but in defiant words declared his own innocence of the charges brought against him because in conscience he had "never been party to any willful error or malice." He ended with an exhortation not to give up the fight. Tyranny could never repress freedom. They were free. Their enemies were slaves. And from the pen of a man whose faith in a Supreme Being remained suspect came a final appeal: "Fight and you will win. God grants victory to the persevering."[13]

In 1812, it was said, God had brought down the first Venezuelan republic with an earthquake. Two years later, Boves and his Legion of Hell destroyed its successor in a campaign that ravished the country. Not even the 80,000-strong followers of Miguel Hidalgo in Mexico in September 1810 had unleashed such destruction or aroused such fears among the populace. The Spaniard José Manuel Oropesa described Venezuela's condition in a graphic passage: "It is no longer a province. . . . The villages are ruined. Whole families have vanished, their only crime that of owning property. . . . In the towns there is neither corn nor fruit. From the churches, everything, even the Holy of Holies, has been stolen."[14]

This was total war. Five years late, in his magnificent address to delegates at the Congress of Angostura, Bolívar would attribute the fall of the first Venezuelan republic to its federalist structure. The reality lay in its weak social base. In the second republic, he had exercised virtual dictatorial power. That government, too, had collapsed, but the reasons proved dramatically different. From the beginning of his return to power in Caracas, he had to confront a far more ominous challenge to the patriot cause—the mobilization of a slave and pardo army nominally in the service of the royalists but with a more menacing agenda and a more determined leader in the person of Boves.

Boves had transformed the military and social character of the Venezuelan conflict. His troops were abler horsemen, soldiers, and lancers than their patriot adversaries. They fought with a fierceness and determination matched only by the bands of Haitian slaves who had committed themselves to end slavery in Saint-Domingue, whatever the cost. In power for a few months in Caracas in 1814, they exercised a form of social democracy devoid of distinctions of rank and color. Ordinary pardos rose to command. Vagrants and beggars were dispatched to work on the haciendas and send food back to the city. Under Boves, the llanero regime inverted the social pyramid. Only the Haitians had gone further in eradicating the debilitating badges of social distinctions.

In his second exile from his beloved Caracas in less than a year, Bolívar had to admit that he could not win the war as long as these people remained the enemy. He had to put together his own pardo army. And he had to articulate a new revolutionary agenda.

The Return to New Granada

In mid-September 1814, accompanied by the redoubtable Mariño and forty-two comrades, Bolívar arrived in Cartagena. He received a hero's welcome. And he savored the moment. In Venezuela some of his former lieutenants denounced him as a traitor and declared him an outlaw. But few in Cartagena blamed him for the collapse of the second republic, and he soon began planning another invasion of his homeland.

More and more he invoked the rhetoric and ideology of the revolutionary with a continental agenda. When Venezuelans and New Granadans quarreled over what he regarded as local or even petty jealousies, he inspired them with compelling words and phrases of the cause he had made his own and now resolved to make theirs as well. Their country was America, a place of no precise boundaries but representing all those who saw their enemies as Spaniards. Their goal was liberty and independence. With such words he resolved to translate the rhetoric of the war into a universal language, truths as self-evident as any inscribed in that Declaration of Independence proclaimed to the world by disaffected British Americans almost forty years earlier.

Victory was inevitably theirs, Bolívar reassured them. Two months before his abrupt departure from Venezuela, he published in the *Gaceta de Caracas* an overview of the Spanish-American cause. "Our revolution," he wrote, referring to the uprisings in Mexico, Peru, Chile, Buenos Aires, New Granada, and Venezuela, "cannot be crushed by force" because these provinces were a "formidable league which cannot be destroyed." And the international situation now appeared to favor them. Among other factors, he noted Great Britain's imminent triumph in the long war with revolutionary France, the reestablishment of the balance of power in Europe, the benefits of U.S. independence to the British, and what its example could mean for the Spanish-American struggle. He ended with a sobering prediction: "What shall we say of our countries, whose political importance will never compare with that of the United States?"[15]

Ironically, a generation of aging North American revolutionary leaders, contemplating the deepening political divisions during the War of 1812, penned similar doubts about the political future of the United States. But in fall 1814 nationalist spirits revived in the aftermath of outrage over the August burning of Washington, D.C. As peace negotiations between the United States and Britain were concluding in Ghent, Belgium, on Christmas Eve, Andrew Jackson, who had led his Tennessee militiamen across the Spanish Florida panhandle, made hasty and controversial preparations to defend the city of New Orleans against an imminent British assault with a makeshift force of white Tennesseans and two free colored battalions, some of whom were refugees from Santo Domingo. When prominent Louisianans voiced objections about the equal treatment Jackson demanded for these troops, Old Hickory responded that they were superb soldiers and added: "They must be for, or against us—distrust them, and you make them your enemies, place confidence in them, and you engage them by every dear and honorable tie to the interest of the country who extends to them equal rights and privileges with white men."[16]

This was a judgment born of expediency as much as conviction. (Two years later, Jackson would be one of the early supporters of the American Colonization Society, whose goal was to address the volatile issue of black and colored participation in civil society by resettling manumitted slaves in Africa.) In time, Bolívar would adopt a similar position about the need to use colored troops and to grant freedom to slaves who joined the patriot force. For the time being, however, he confronted in New Granada a different problem—a civil war in which the majority of the patriot population insistently subordinated local and provincial interests to Bolívar's continental exhortations. Though he received a warm welcome on his arrival in Tunja, capital of the United Provinces, the outpourings of praise were for him more than the cause he professed. As a consolation, perhaps, his appeal prompted the Congress to provide him with a new army and the charge of laying siege to the most defiant of New Granada's provinces—Cundinamarca.

In its mountainous villages and especially in Santafé de Bogotá, Bolívar was more feared than admired. The archbishop of the city had excommunicated him; its civic leaders denounced him as the Man of Terror. In his march through the province Bolívar tried to allay their fears by sparing captured prisoners. There would be no war to the death in this campaign. The city's leaders remained suspicious, however, and for two days held out against the invaders. On December 12, 1814, the Liberator entered for the first time the city Alexander von Humboldt had called the Athens of South America.

In the early days of his rule, the Man of Terror carried out his admittedly firm governance of the city in a manner that reassured some of his harshest critics. He pledged respect and security for the political rights of the citizenry. The church set aside its decree of excommunication, and Bolívar dutifully attended the ceremony for national unity in the cathedral. He urged deserters to rejoin the war against the royalist redoubts in the south and on the coast. Throughout he demanded sacrifice and commitment. "War is the epitome of all evil," he reminded a weary populace, "but tyranny is the substance of all war."[17]

These were anything but reassuring words. And neither time nor circumstances favored Bolívar for what he had in mind to unite New Granadans. In the south, a royalist force from Pasto took Popayán province. In Spain the restored monarch Ferdinand VII succumbed under pressure from a stubborn minority of absolutists (the "servile ones") and repudiated the constitution of 1812. In February 1815 the king elected to crush the American rebellion that had erupted five years before in his name. He dispatched an armada of fifty ships and 10,000 men (many of them veterans of the long struggle against Napoleon) and commanded by one of his best generals, Pablo Morillo. In April the "army of pacification" disembarked in Venezuela, easily recaptured the last rebel stronghold in the country (Margarita Island), and marched gloriously into Caracas. From there Morillo made preparations for the invasion of New Granada.[18]

In the meantime, Bolívar endured further setbacks, most of them attributable to the jealousies he instinctively aroused and the fractious character of New Granadan politics. Determined to subdue the royalist town of Santa Marta on the north coast, Bolívar marched his troops down from the mountainous interior, liberating river ports and reopening the links between the interior and the coast. He had made this conquering journey before, in late 1812 and early 1813; only then he had carried it out in reverse and in circumstances more favorable to the cause. This time he desperately needed the cooperation of the civic leaders of Cartagena. The city's military commander of Cartagena, Manuel del Castillo, was no royalist, but he was virulently anti-Bolívar. In a series of broadsides Castillo denounced Bolívar as a coward and an incompetent. Cartagena's elders offered their assistance, but only if Bolívar agreed to what was for him unthinkable: to yield command of his army to Castillo. Privately, they feared a victorious Bolívar would install a dictatorship and restore the War to the Death decree. In desperation, Bolívar elected to lay siege to the fortified city. The decision provoked the hatred of its inhabitants, who refused to supply his soldiers with food and who poisoned the water supply by dumping dead animals into the wells.

Only then did Bolívar relinquish his command, and in a letter (May 8) to the president of the United Provinces of New Granada, he offered what his critics doubtless believed was a lame excuse for the military setback: Cartagena's true patriots had succumbed to those willing to compromise. Despite the widespread ignorance of the masses about their rights and interests, "every thinking person" preferred independence. The key to victory, he predicted, ultimately lay with Great Britain and the willingness of British leaders to recognize how much the independence of Spanish America would benefit British commerce and political interests and the harm a royalist triumph would do to those interests. His continued presence in the region, he believed, would only deepen the hatreds and divisions in the city and lead to further disasters. He chose to leave the country where he stood accused as the perpetrator of many of its misfortunes and dishonor. He added a self-exculpatory qualification, "my only share therein would be to have been the first victim of them."[19]

That same day he embarked on a ship into the Caribbean.

The Caribbean Experience

Bolívar arrived in Kingston, Jamaica, with little money and even less prospect of drawing on his Venezuelan assets. The island harbored smugglers, Spanish Americans still supportive of the patriot cause, and, most important, British sympathizers, and he determined to rely on their goodwill and financial support to renew the struggle. This would be no easy task, given the recent setbacks to the cause and stories about his abrupt departure from New Granada. But Bolívar possessed well-developed social skills and had proved to be an exceptional literary stylist, and over the next seven months he made good use of both to rally support and funding for a struggle he passionately believed would inevitably triumph.

He was especially solicitous of Maxwell Hyslop, a British merchant who might provide financial support and (Bolívar presumed) might have influence with powerful people in British society. In Bolívar's mind, British political and especially commercial interests lay with the triumph of the independence movement. In one of his numerous letters to Hyslop, he went so far as to suggest the cession to Britain of the provinces of Panamá and Nicaragua—the first a largely indifferent spectator to the New Granadan war, the second a dependency of New Spain (Mexico). In return for its "insignificant" investment (one million pounds sterling, 20,000 or 30,000 rifles, munitions, and volunteers), the British would easily recoup the cost by opening up a free Spanish America to its commerce and at the same time London would prevent continental Europeans from making "another Europe in America."[20]

In this and other letters written during his stay on the island, Bolívar exhibited all the traits of the dreamer and strategist, the exiled leader imagining a portentous role for his America in a transatlantic world still reeling from the horrendous losses and costs of a war that had begun when he was ten years old. His mood in these months often vacillated between commitment and despair. "I am disposed to do anything for my country," he wrote another confidant, Luis Brión, "but I am living in uncertainty and despair." To the president of the United Provinces of New Granada he rejoiced that Napoleon's defeat at Waterloo (June 18) had effectively liberated Europe. He grimly speculated that the war would continue if rumors of Napoleon's plan to seek asylum in America in order to restore his empire were true. The armies of Europe would follow him, and in desperation the British would blockade "all America."[21]

This was both prognosis and fantasy. The British exiled Napoleon to the island of St. Helena in the south Atlantic Ocean, but Bolívar had correctly perceived that Britain was Spanish America's only reliable benefactor. In early September he made yet another appeal to the British community on the island. The Jamaica Letter was more than a plea for aid. In it, Bolívar crafted his most damning indictment of the Spanish for their centuries of misrule in the Americas. "That wicked stepmother," he wrote, "is the source of all our suffering." Everywhere in Spanish America, he continued in his accusatory literary voice, those who loved liberty had resisted the assault on their liberties and rights. How could Europe ignore such entreaties? Did Europeans wish Spanish America to disappear? In the end he employed the familial refrain of the orphan whose future remained an uncertainty. The

French invasion of the Iberian peninsula, he believed, left Spanish Americans "unsure of our future destiny and threatened by anarchy for lack of a legitimate, just and liberal government." In such circumstances, he averred, the only course was to plunge "headlong into the chaos of revolution."[22]

The Jamaica Letter is a fundamental statement in the rich repository of Bolivarian texts—eloquent, defiant, and in some passages a despairing defense of continental independence and a fervent plea for assistance from Great Britain and even from the United States, where in some political circles he was already becoming a figure of admiration. In his analysis of the Spanish American past and its likely future, he could be remarkably perceptive. Spanish Americans, he wrote in prophetic words, were neither European nor Indian but a people striving to regain their rights against the Spanish oppressors, though he neglected to affirm the rights of the continent's indigenous population. By implication if not by conviction he regarded both Creole and indigenous person as victim. In words that the esteemed Cuban poet and revolutionary José Martí often cited, Bolívar called for governing institutions that reflected local conditions and habits rather than the inappropriate models from Europe or North America. His doubts about the preparation of a people for republican government persisted. "We are dominated by the vices that one learns under the rule of a nation like Spain," he confessed. "Is it conceivable that a newly emancipated people can soar to the heights of liberty. . . . There is no reasonable probability to bolster our hopes."[23]

In keeping with his well-established skepticism about federal government, he called for a strong executive, principally because Spanish Americans lacked experience in self-governance. He proposed a continental bond in a league of former Spanish colonies, and in a continuing passage recognized fundamental differences among the provinces then in rebellion, predicting the creation of seventeen independent countries carved out of Spanish America. History has largely validated his optimistic comments on the future of liberalism in Chile and his sobering comments about its record in neighboring Peru. Echoing Miranda, he called for a union of Venezuela and New Granada into the nation of Colombia with a government modeled on the British example, though here again he expressed doubts about its workability because of New Granadans' fascination with federalism.

The contrasting Chilean-Peruvian example proved to be more than an incidental comparison. He chose Chile as a likely prospect for an enduring liberal republic because of its climate and, as he perceived its demographic makeup, the uniformity of its climate and its people. Peru, plagued by the corrupting effects of gold and slaves, he predicted, would never achieve the stature of an independent Chile. The Peruvian aristocracy would never accept democracy, and its slaves and pardos would always reject aristocratic rule. In such comments, he wrote his epitaph for an independent Spanish America. But in the final passages of the Jamaica Letter, he invoked some of the noblest sentiments of the revolutionary age in the Americas—a passionate appeal for unity, a firm belief in the eventual triumph of the war of independence, and visions of a happy and prosperous future for a people liberated from a corrupt government. With such convictions, who could doubt that "unity was the only thing" necessary to win the struggle in order to "establish a powerful empire with a free government and benevolent laws?"[24]

In this appeal, both the eloquence of his words and the logic of his argument failed to induce the British to act. The explanation lay not so much in the weakness of his argument as in London's memory of its choices in earlier rebellions and civil wars. In 1775, the British had calculated that the political convulsions in the North Atlantic seaboard colonies must be met with a firm response, but they had erred in their belief that British-American society replicated that of England. By the time they recognized the possibilities of exploiting the latent animosities of poor whites, Indians, and African Americans against the patriot white elite and shifted the war against the rebels to the southern colonies, U.S. emissaries had signed treaties of alliance and commerce with the French and obtained subsidies and loans from several European countries. In 1793, the British again miscalculated by dispatching an army into strife-ridden French Saint-Domingue, where the eruption of a colored revolt in the aftermath of the French Revolution had in turn precipitated a black slave uprising that menaced both white and colored. Five years later, the commanding British leader, Thomas Maitland, negotiated what was in effect an admission of error in intervening in a conflict of uncertain outcome.

They did not intend to make the same mistake again. But they would shortly elect not to assist or even permit the Spanish and their putative European allies to reconquer Spanish America. Even in the precarious months of late 1815 and early 1816, as royalist forces overwhelmed patriot defenders everywhere in Spanish America save in faraway Buenos Aires, the most perceptive British observers calculated that the war would go on and that inevitably Spain would lose her New World empire. But neither did this mean they would commit themselves to intervening in what they correctly saw (as did their U.S. counterparts) as a civil war in which the exhaustion of both sides seemed preferable to an unqualified victory by either participant.

That was an astute and certainly politic perception, but it blinded both British and U.S. leaders to what they were witnessing in the Spanish-American struggle and especially in the character and determination of Bolívar. In the

Jamaica Letter, he had described the adversaries in a civil war as conservative and reformer. In another passage, he noted that individuals may accomplish much in the fervor of revolutionary change. The rebel may ultimately suffer defeat or give up the battle or be willing to compromise; the reformers presumably had gotten what they wanted in the liberal passages of the constitution of 1812 and perhaps yearned only for its restoration. But for the revolutionary, even for one who wishes to restore only ancient privileges and liberties, there is always something more to be done, even in the darkest moments of the struggle. And in the months following his writing of the Jamaica Letter, Bolívar continued with his epistolary broadsides to island newspapers. At one point, he considered sailing for England to make a personal appeal for assistance. By the end of the year, however, his spirits again sank. Momentarily, they revived with news that the leaders of besieged Cartagena wanted him to return to save them from Morillo's army. En route, he learned of the city's collapse. He now elected to change course. He determined to go to the only place in the Caribbean where he could find the assistance he desperately needed: Haiti.

Bolívar landed in Aux Cayes in the Haitian republic on Christmas Eve, 1815, and arrived in the capital of Port-au-Prince on New Year's Day, 1816. The following day, he met with the president, Alexandre Pétion, son of a French father and African mother and veteran of the war against the French invaders. Pétion was the leader of Colored Haiti, a republican enterprise of small farmers and limited commercial contact with Europe. To the north, in what was North Province, lay Black Haiti, an enemy kingdom commanded by another veteran of the slave revolt, Henri Christophe, who had crowned himself Henri I and ordered the construction of a formidable citadel on the northern coast to shield against another mythical invasion of white infidels bent on reimposing the slave regime.

In 1816 both Haitis were pariah states, unrecognized by European nations and, understandably, by the United States, but by virtue of entitlement Pétion belonged to an elite class of Haitians who would have understood Bolívar's cause and his resentments about the ill treatment of American Spaniards by the motherland. And he correctly sensed Bolívar needed a benefactor. Of course he knew the risks. The eastern portion of the island was a Spanish colony, and the U.S. government and most of the governments of Europe, save possibly that of Great Britain, would be suspicious of any Haitian aid to the Spanish-American cause.

In any event, Bolívar had no other place to go, and when Pétion laid down the only condition for refitting his army—a pledge to emancipate the slaves in every province he liberated—Bolívar agreed. After all, he could word the decree, as did Abraham Lincoln half a century later, in such a way as to aid the patriot cause yet maintain his fellow Creoles' belief that in granting slaves their freedom in exchange for fighting under a patriot banner they would not be agreeing to social equality. The Haitians had already made that choice. In the earliest days of independence, the state had abolished social rank and privilege founded on color, status, occupation, or condition. Put differently, human rights superseded civil rights. This was fundamentally different than the reform of a political and social system. It was a revolutionary act. But its implications went much further.

Bolívar could not afford to dwell on such matters during these days. In early June 1816, when he stepped ashore on the Venezuelan coast, he fulfilled his pledge to Pétion by granting freedom to any slave who joined the patriot cause. Understandably, he qualified the decree with the statement that those slaves (and their families) who refused to join would remain in bondage, yet even this concession failed to benefit the patriot cause and served only to increase Creole fears about a racial war. If anything, the decree (and a subsequent declaration) motivated slaves to join the royalist camp and, more disturbingly, did little initially to swell patriot ranks with slave recruits.

But Bolívar recognized that there could be no turning back to the old way of raising a patriot army, not even after he suffered a humiliating defeat at the battle of Ocumare in his first effort to assault the Venezuelan coast from his Haitian base. In the aftermath of that disaster, when some of his generals complained of his unworthiness as a commander and even conspired against him, Bolívar deftly employed the emancipation decrees to gain more support from Pétion. In December 1816, following a year of frustration and disappointment (and a failed assassination plot against him during his stay in Kingston), he once again set foot on Venezuelan soil, determined not only to liberate his homeland but persuaded that he must now wage a new kind of war with an army of Creoles, pardos, and slaves against seasoned veterans from Spain.

With such convictions he voiced the commitment of the American revolutionary, not the anger of the Venezuelan rebel. He now asked how as well as why he would wage this battle. On the eve of what would be a triumphal decade of struggle during which his reputation soared on both sides of the Atlantic, he was not certain if this mighty army of liberation he proposed to create could be contained in an apocalyptic violence he aptly described as the chaos of revolution. More troublesome, he was unsure if the people of color he mobilized to create a new republican order would subordinate what he believed was their instinctive racial identity to nation and unity. That was one of the most fundamental questions of the revolutionary age in the Americas and one of its most troubling legacies.

CHAPTER FOUR

~

The Liberator

In these uncertain circumstances, Bolívar commenced a war for the second liberation of Venezuela. This time, his purpose would be not one of restoration but a different crusade and with a different army. Although he confronted the reality of a continent largely under royalist control, he did have certain advantages. The first was his passionate devotion to a cause, however doubtful he was about the capabilities of the people he now pledged to liberate to take on the responsibilities of a republic. The second was Spanish—or, more precisely, royal—stupidity in believing that a generation of Creoles who had begun a fight to reaffirm old privileges or who had fundamentally rejected any notion of sharing power with people of color would relent before a sanguinary and relentless Spanish counterattack. Beyond that, there were only improbabilities. A goodly number of his fellow Creoles, remembering what had happened in the overthrow of the first republic, expressed doubts about his intentions. They had too many examples of what might go wrong. Bolívar tried to allay their fears with arguments both self-serving and disingenuous, but at bottom, as he well knew, without the support of people of color and armed slaves promised their freedom there could be no victory. In victory, there would be uncertainty; without victory, there would be only the certainty of a world that could never be restored.

So, he learned to turn every argument against how he intended to fight the war on its head. When pressed by Pétion about desertions or the numbers of slaves who went over to the royalist cause, Bolívar responded that they were ignorant and unaware of their true interests. Pétion, a man of color, would understand the subtlety of his words because he had faced a similar dilemma during the Haitian struggle. To his comrade and vice president Santander and those who believed that black slaves would not commit their lives to fight a "white man's war"—an oblique reference to the persistent rumor that in battle soldiers of color on both sides aimed their rifles not at colored but at white combatants on the other side—Bolívar retorted that those "accustomed to hardship and fatigue" were "men for whom death can have little less meaning than life."[1]

In far less perilous circumstances, Washington had come to a similar conclusion when he recognized that social marginals more than militiamen were likelier to stay the course. Among the ranks of black slaves and pardos Bolívar rarely used such language, but to wary Venezuelan slaveholders or to his New Granadan allies intent on preserving white privilege he could be blunt. In 1820, when the issue continued to divide white Venezuelans, he invoked language both enlightened and what we might classify as racist. "Is it fair that only free men should die for the liberation of slaves?" Or, was it not "proper that the slaves should acquire their rights on the battlefield and that their dangerous numbers should be lessened by a process both just and effective?" Always, the Venezuelan experience remained fixed in his mind. There, free people had died and slaves had survived. Perhaps it was not a "prudent" choice to use slaves, he informed Santander, referring to a decision made about patriot military operations in Cundinamarca, but not to arm them meant "they will outlive us again."[2]

This was a realistic, even cynical, assessment about the role of slaves as well as the castas in the war. His reasoning although not his purpose contrasted with the views of a career royalist officer with considerable experience in Venezuela, José de Cevallos, who had written the king in July 1815 urging the restoration of rights granted to the castas in the Cádiz constitution—admission to the universities and to religious communities, and the right to receive holy orders to those who served the nation. In Venezuela, the question was of utmost importance. Without the restoration of such privileges, the castas would become more alienated. The only way to curb their violent behavior was to treat them as no less deserving than white Venezuelans. "For these men," he wrote, meaning pardos, "giving them that which one fears they want to grab will satisfy them and cure the evil in their own race."[3]

This strategy offered the best chance of victory, Cevallos believed. But the Spanish king listened to those who called for a campaign of pacification. When Morillo arrived, Cevallos lost influence and returned to Spain. Many of the llaneros who had fought with Boves shifted their loyalty to the patriot cause. Bolívar had made the expedient decision for winning the war.

Changing Strategies

No leader of the hemispheric wars of independence had framed the argument for mobilizing slaves or the parallel issue of employing colored troops in such stark and disturbing language. Had Bolívar assessed more closely what had happened in Saint-Domingue when whites and coloreds had collided, and the African slaves had sensed an opportunity to make a breach in the institution of slavery, he might have listened more attentively to the warnings coming from Santander. In any event, a more immediate problem for him in 1817 was the fractured character of his command. The experience of defeat in the first two Venezuelan republics had taught him a fundamental lesson—to win, he must enlist not only colored and mestizo soldiers from the countryside but also those who led them, men such as the pardo Manuel Piar or Santiago Mariño, who had accompanied Bolívar in the retreat from Caracas in 1814 but whose envy of the Liberator raised doubts about his willingness to accept a subordinate role. And then there was the mestizo José Antonio Páez, an illiterate llanero, a sometime merchant, sometime cowboy proficient at both horsemanship and killing. Of the three, Páez proved the most reliable in the Venezuelan war. Bolívar's junior by seven years, he had weathered the tumultuous local wars of the Apure River region and with unrivaled ability and bravado had put together an army of fierce llanero warriors, some of them veterans of Boves's royalist force. More than anyone, Páez taught Bolívar an invaluable lesson about leadership: To command such men, you must prove yourself to them.[4]

These three men came from the countryside, and to unite them firmly to the patriot cause Bolívar chose to alter his wartime strategy. The decision was a matter of political expediency as well. Instead of focusing on the recovery of Caracas, which had cost him another defeat, he elected to march into Guayana province, which straddled the lower Orinoco and thus provided a valuable outlet to the Atlantic and desperately needed supply lines. Piar had already laid siege to the river town of Angostura (now Ciudad Bolívar), and with Bolívar's fresh troops and with the support of schooners and brigantines, the patriots succeeded in taking control of the city in mid-July 1817. The victory was as sweet as any Bolívar had experienced in the Admirable Campaign. Throughout, he had endured virtually every privation those who followed him had suffered. He was learning to adapt.

At the moment of victory he was haunted by intrigue and conspiracy within his own fragile command. The initial challenge came from Mariño, whose unwillingness to serve in a subordinate role had prompted him to lead a small group in the creation of a reformist government in which he, not Bolívar, became supreme commander. The movement quickly collapsed when Bolívar denounced the participants (some of whom professed to be his friends), and Mariño took refuge on Margarita Island. A second threat came from the pardo Piar, who like Mariño felt aggrieved by the Liberator's assertiveness in assuming command of the Guayana campaign. Over the course of several months, Piar became more and more outspoken and even obstinate, in part out of jealousy and, it was rumored, out of conviction that white Creole officers remained indifferent to the growing social demands of the pardos. Pleading ill health, Piar resigned his command.

The suspicions about his motives did not abate. In summer 1817, a year after the first emancipation decree, Bolívar confronted another wartime crisis, this time involving racial divisions within patriot ranks. Informed by two officers that Piar was plotting an insurrection, or perhaps even a race war, Bolívar summoned the pardo officer to his headquarters. Piar fled. He was hunted down and brought to Angostura, where an impromptu war council indicted him for insurrection, desertion, and treason. The sentence was death. Most of Bolívar's officers believed that he would commute the sentence: Piar, regardless of what he had done or might do, was a brave soldier and widely popular among his troops. Surely a death sentence would incite an insurrection.

Bolívar remained unmoved. The entire affair had a chilling effect among patriot ranks throughout Venezuela, inspiring awe at Bolívar's resolve but never completely silencing the persistent rumors of racial animosity and envy the Liberator held about a man who was his equal as a commander. Not surprisingly, Bolívar later contributed to the criticism and defense of his conduct when he wrote that "the death of General Piar was a political necessity which saved the country." And what of General Mariño, equally insubordinate and by Bolívar's admission who "also deserved to die"? Mariño escaped the firing squad. He made his obligatory acknowledgment of the Liberator's authority and in time regained his command. Bolívar justified his pardon of Mariño on humanitarian grounds, but the fundamental reason was political or, more accurately, racial. Mariño was white and could be forgiven. To execute him for crimes similar to those committed by the pardo Piar would have signaled to the Liberator's Creole allies that he was unwilling to draw a color line.[5]

For the Venezuelan campaign, Bolívar had to rely on Páez, who may have had little comprehension of the Liberator's continental vision but intuitively understood how to win the war in the Venezuelan countryside. On New Year's Eve 1817, Bolívar led a 3,000-man force almost 300 miles into the forbidding Venezuelan plains. There he struck a bargain with Páez: If the llaneros committed to the revolution, he would grant them land. For the time being, that promise proved sufficient to mobilize them against Morillo's troops, but Páez was too savvy to deny his followers their habit of making war for booty or to lead them out of the Apure plains. For them the war remained a local and often personal conflict, only now those who disdained them were not the white Creoles but white royalists. Bolívar began to woo Páez by sending him much-needed supplies. Initially suspicious of this Creole interloper, Páez ultimately acquiesced in Bolívar's plea to join forces. They met for the first time in early 1818, and the illiterate llanero chieftain readily acknowledged Bolívar as a true warrior, a man unafraid.[6]

By incorporating these fierce warriors from the countryside, Bolívar the elite Creole broadened the social base of his army. The decision reflected that symbiotic blend of idealism and pragmatism in his thinking about what was necessary to nourish a sense of loyalty and identity with the patriot cause among disparate social and racial groups from the countryside. He knew the risk, but there was no other way to replenish his command. He had employed similar reasoning to justify his decision to offer freedom to those slaves who committed to the patriot cause. These decisions had limited success, and they also had fearful consequences, as Bolívar discovered in the last tormented years of his life. But the passions and ideals behind them ultimately became part of the lore of Bolivarian mythology. As Rousseau had written, explaining Rome's strength, the nation depended not on the weaklings of the city but the tribes of the countryside.[7]

Ambivalent Signals from the United States

In these and other decisions, Bolívar demonstrated resolve, but some U.S. leaders began to express doubts that Bolívar and the cause he led represented a Spanish-American variation of their revolution. From a transatlantic perspective, undeniably, the widespread denunciations of the French invasion of Iberia and the later declarations of loyalty to the deposed Ferdinand or independence throughout Spanish America appeared to mirror the experience of British American protest, rebellion, and revolution. Their eruption revived hopeful discussion among North Americans about the future of republican government in the mainland Americas and a parallel apprehension among others about rebellion and revolution in the Caribbean.

These issues resonated differently when assessed from a hemispheric perspective. At the onset of the Spanish-American wars of independence, among North Americans it is possible to identify two contemporary perspectives on the hemispheric future, each with its respective proponents. Those of the first category believed in a weak but nonetheless tangible unity among governments throughout the hemisphere acting in the spirit of "good neigh-borliness" as the best hope for preserving republican government and inde-pendence. Their proponents drew on the lingering revolutionary sentiments about a hemispheric America arrayed against European monarchy. Those of the second emphasized the continuing dangers of European (principally Brit-ish and French) meddling in the weak outposts of the Spanish empire—one of which was Florida—and the related question of slave rebellion and the role of people of color in warring armies.

Bolívar's name figured frequently among both groups. To those of the first, he symbolized the republican advocate, enemy of monarchy, and lib-erator. Those in the second group were more concerned with Bolívar's de-cision to arm the slaves and his increasing reliance on people of color in his army. The distinctions were not always so clear, and in the uncertainties of the patriot struggle after 1815 and the often fierce debates over U.S. policy toward the Spanish-American patriot cause, sorting out the two can be dif-ficult. Secretary of State John Quincy Adams and Henry Clay (then in the Congress), for example, occupied opposite camps in the debate over rec-ognition in 1817 and 1818. (Adams expressed reservations about Bolívar's arming of slave troops; Clay defended Bolívar's policy.) Seven years later, when Adams was president and Clay secretary of state, they were ideologi-cal allies as Congress debated the U.S. role in hemispheric affairs. Andrew Jackson, contrastingly, believed the United States should have little of-ficial involvement with hemispheric organizations, but he would have led an army to defend Spanish America from European invasion. Briefly stated, the debates within the U.S. government over the Spanish-American wars in the decade after 1815 compelled political leaders to articulate a national rather than a hemispheric position.

Not surprisingly, the attitudes of the second camp appeared to dominate contemporary discussions about the U.S. relationship to the Spanish-American wars of independence and particularly toward Bolívar. After the War of 1812, the U.S. government increasingly distanced itself as the North American kindred spirit of the revolutionary movements in Span-ish America. Among modern Latin Americans, this shift is often attributed to the desire of U.S. leaders to take advantage of a struggle to advance its own commercial interests, its continental ambitions in Spanish Florida, and frankly as justification for its own imperial designs in the hemisphere. Unde-niably, that is part of the story, but it is not the whole story. Criticism of U.S. "indifference" to the Spanish-American cause persisted, not only among the Creoles but in the U.S. Congress as well. Bolívar himself joined the ranks of the grumblers about Washington's lukewarm expressions of friendship. He was reluctant to acknowledge that the September 1815 U.S. declaration of neutrality and recognition of belligerency effectively benefited the insurgents because it permitted their ships to use U.S. ports. This and other nuances of the relationship—especially the contraband trade with the rebels emanating from several U.S. ports—generated little enthusiasm for the United States among Venezuelans. Bolívar consistently turned down official requests from Washington that he make restitution for goods his privateers seized from U.S. vessels.

What Bolívar wanted—indeed, desperately needed—was U.S. recognition, and he had ample reason to believe that the public sympathies for the patriot cause among North Americans, especially in the coastal cities and in the trans-Appalachian southwestern states, would prompt the administration to act. Several western congressmen, notably Clay, became more insistent in making the case for extending recognition. The pressure grew strong enough to prompt President James Monroe (who had earlier expressed public sympathy for the Spanish-American rebels) to authorize a special three-member commission to Spanish America to assess the war, to determine what form of government might result from a rebel victory, and to explain U.S. neutrality. The ninth item of the emissaries' instructions referred specifically to the controversial issue of color: "It might be useful to know, whether any and what connection exists between this chief, and the chiefs or rulers at St. Domingo [Haiti]; also the number of negroes in arms."[8]

In assessing this mission into a war zone, Adams—future president and, in his postpresidential career in Congress, fierce antagonist of the extension of slavery—had more on his mind than a response to those in Congress insisting on recognition of the new republics to the south and, particularly, the government's posture toward Bolívar and what he represented. For Adams, and the revolutionary generation he spoke for, Bolívar's military tactics and the personalism he injected into his command were uncomfortable reminders about the political turbulence within the country increasingly identified with Jackson and the democratic fervor Old Hickory aroused. Adams was a nationalist and expansionist, as was Jackson, but the nationalism of Jackson sprang from more visceral and democratic emotions.

As did Bolívar, Jackson understood the need to incorporate people of color into a military campaign and to provide them a place in the political and social order. After all, the battle for Spanish Florida went beyond strategic questions. Since colonial days, its remoteness and weak Spanish control had made it a haven for runaway slaves and Seminole Indians, who collectively repulsed a U.S. invasion in 1812 and for fifteen years after Florida's annexation (1819) tied up a U.S. military in the Seminole Wars. After he had become president Adams voiced concerns that Bolívar might mobilize his army of black and pardo troops for an invasion of the Spanish Caribbean, particularly Cuba, but in spring 1818, the Spanish believed the more dangerous threat to Cuba came not from Bolívar but from Jackson, who reputedly was planning to coordinate an invasion of the island with a rumored Cuban slave insurrection.[9]

Since he had departed the presidency, John Quincy Adams's father had more or less written off the first postrevolutionary generation as either indifferent or ungrateful for the accomplishments of the generation of 1776. As secretary of state the son had a different problem: he had to stanch the growing sentiments in Congress and in the public for the Spanish-American cause and at the same time not make himself politically irrelevant. He commenced with what was to him a largely accurate description of the stages in the coming of the American Revolution—first, a justifiable demand for colonial rights; and second, a declaration of independence—and followed with the disdainful and misleading remark that the struggle in Spanish America lacked "neither unity of cause nor unity of effort." Those privy to George Washington's somber views about the course of the American Revolution during the Valley Forge winter of 1777–1778 might have set him straight about the disturbing social fissures the war brought on. The Spanish-American convulsions, he continued, had commenced as civil war. He was particularly disturbed by Bolívar's decree freeing those slaves who fought under the patriot banner, a move thus prompting Adams to ask rhetorically in late 1817 whether the "cause of Venezuela is precisely the same as ours was."[10]

In truth, Adams's assessment of the Spanish-American wartime condition proved to be as distorted as Bolívar's judgments about U.S. policy. Adams was largely correct in his description of the struggle as a civil war and thus warranting a circumspect neutrality. It had begun as a civil conflict, but in the course of seven years it had become something more, and Bolívar had been instrumental in that transformation. Adams erred in his unwillingness to acknowledge that Bolívar's decision to emancipate those slaves who joined the patriot cause was not so much a matter of conviction as a necessity for fighting a successful campaign. In comparing the two wars, Adams had distorted some uncomfortable realities about the American Revolution, particularly the guerrilla character of the war in the southern colonies, but his pessimistic assessment of the wars in Spanish America reinforced the opponents of recognition.

In early 1818, Congress took up the question, and from the onset of the debate, how Bolívar was fighting the war became a central issue. Henry

Clay, outspoken in his support of recognition of the new republics, chose Venezuela as his example. He noted the extenuating circumstances Bolívar confronted—the deep social and racial divisions within the country and the "execrable outrages" committed on the patriots by slaves armed by the Spanish. "Could it be believed," Clay responded to a member's outcry about the War to the Death decree and Bolívar's bloody retaliation, "if the slaves had been let loose upon us in the south . . . that General Washington would not have resorted to retribution?"[11]

Washington had not issued such a decree because the divisions and fragmentation within the American Revolution rarely approached the severity of those in Venezuela. Yet in actions if not declaration Washington sometimes imposed severe retribution for those who indirectly aided the British. In 1779, in the aftermath of the harsh Valley Forge winter, the victory at Saratoga, and the forging of the French alliance, he launched a scorched-earth campaign against those tribes of the Iroquois Confederacy who had thrown in their lot with the enemy. Years later, the mention of Washington's name was a fearful reminder of the savagery of this assault among the New York Iroquois. Such tales about how the nation's first commander in chief had resorted to guerrilla warfare proved insufficient to move the seemingly implacable Adams to embrace the Spanish-American patriot cause and the man who was leading it. The truth of the matter, as Adams himself bitterly acknowledged, was that Spanish-American agents bought and outfitted ships, raised moneys, purchased arms, and recruited sailors in New Orleans and every U.S. port on the Atlantic coast in defiance of neutrality law.[12]

The gravamen of the issue, as most U.S. leaders saw it, was Bolívar's decision to use slave troops and the numbers of pardos in his army. Although Adams had little sympathy with slaveowners or slavery, he understood the sentiments of those who feared slave revolt. He was not a racist and had little to do with the American Colonization Society, founded in 1817 to encourage manumission and the emigration of freed slaves to Africa and Haiti. After he left the presidency, he became an enemy of the "slave power" and for years fought against it as a Massachusetts congressman. In time, as it did among other nineteenth-century U.S. political leaders—among them, Abraham Lincoln—his racial attitudes would soften. But despite this transformation of both mind and spirit, Adams retained unto his death doubts and apprehensions that the means Bolívar had chosen to win the victory was fraught with danger. In the decade after 1815, there was a danger from without, undeniably, from a European alliance to restore Spanish rule, but there was also a perceived danger of another "revolution from below," perhaps not as menacing as that in Haiti but troubling nonetheless to those increasingly wary of the kind of war Bolívar had chosen to wage. North Americans of differing political views had celebrated Bolívar's resolve and persistence in the struggle to achieve the liberation of Spanish America from Spanish rule. They understood the strategic implications of the war he waged. But as they dwelled more and more on the makeup of his army and his style of governance, they began to ask themselves, "Is he one of us?"

What U.S. (and British) leaders failed to perceive was that Bolívar desperately wanted to be accepted as a transatlantic player in the game of international politics. What Bolívar did not understand was that to U.S. and European leaders, international politics was no game. And in Bolívar they began to see why some of his comrades had become troubled about the way he was fighting the war. He was a dangerous man. If he won, that would serve U.S. and British interests, but there would remain the task of taming him.

The Grand Design

Although Bolívar complained more and more about U.S. policies and official indifference to the patriot struggle, he had more immediate problems in fighting the war. In the early months of 1818 he carried out a haphazard campaign of hit-and-run war with his Spanish adversary, General Pablo Morillo. Bolívar now possessed the numerical advantage on the Venezuelan battlefield, but at a time when he desperately wanted to take advantage of a weakened and increasingly frustrated enemy, his llanero warriors more and more resisted his insistent demands for discipline. In their own minds, they were allies fighting alongside his soldiers. Their passions were liberty and freedom, but they defined these words differently than Bolívar, and they had a narrower conception of nation. Their leader was Páez, who advocated wearing the enemy down when Bolívar called for destroying him.

Bolívar had already begun to deal with this problem. He fashioned a unified command structure whereby regional leaders (*caudillos*) had the choice of either accepting his authority (and becoming generals) or running the risk of punishment, isolation, or, as in the case of Piar, execution. In a decree of September 1817, the arrangement took on a formal and more professional character with the creation of a general staff and by 1819 the formation of three armies—of the East, the West, and the Center, the last commanded by Bolívar himself. At the same time he looked increasingly to Europe and Britain for seasoned and more disciplined soldiers to bolster his army. Circumstances favored him. In the years after the long war against the French, the British had mustered out more than 30,000 men. Merchants had stockpiled uniforms and arms unsalable in continental markets. With little money to either hire mercenaries or purchase matériel, Bolívar's emissary in London simply doled out promissory notes to the suppliers and sent the ne'er-do-well veterans on the next ship to Venezuela. When they arrived and met the Liberator, he handed out promotions to the officers and pledged to pay them what they had received in the British army.[13]

From the beginning the entire project was fraught with disappointment, and worse. Some of the freshly promoted colonels seemed more interested in the pomp and circumstance of a peacetime service. Others carried on petty quarrels with one another. Some even conspired against Bolívar. Still others succumbed to tropical diseases—yellow fever, smallpox, and malaria—or complained endlessly about the meager food ration or cursed the hardships of survival in an environment relentlessly unforgiving and among people they found both hostile and unappreciative. One of their number, Colonel A. E. Hippisley, became so disgusted when Bolívar refused a promotion that he returned to England, where he spent his remaining years spewing out his venom in print and words against the Liberator.

But for every one of the detractors, there was an admirer, and none more adulatory than Daniel O'Leary, who became Bolívar's aide-de-camp, collaborator, preserver of his papers, and biographer. Bolíver often reminisced that the legionnaires—some 4,000 Europeans and a much smaller number from the United States—proved vital to the patriot cause. That was arguable, but what remained a certainty in his mind was the fact that their participation signaled to a doubtful European and especially an ambivalent British public that the Spanish-American cause was something more than a civil war within the Spanish empire. Their presence, he believed, was a reminder to the world and particularly to the U.S. government that the patriot struggle would go on.[14]

In early 1819 he set forth a higher purpose to the war, a statement more detailed than the proverbial U.S. Declaration of Independence. His army constituted a liberating force, but from 1817 its authority derived from emergency measures. The "restored" Venezuelan republic, he instinctively knew, would remain spiritually if not legally homeless until he articulated its identity. That was the challenge he met when in mid-February 1819 he delivered one of his most memorable addresses to twenty-six delegates of the Venezuelan congress in the Orinoco River village of Angostura, a speech about their future and his.

The Angostura address was one of the milestones in the Bolivarian parade on the revolutionary stage, an admission of the severe measures he had taken and affirmation that he must live by their judgment of his record. He was the Liberator, their chief, and thus an instrument of their will. To that end, he submitted an outline for a constitution of what would become the unified Colombian republic—composed of Venezuela, New Granada, and Quito—and in the same passage admitted that a union of such disparate provinces might very well be impracticable. There could be no retreat from the path they had chosen. Separation from Spain, he believed, was analogous to the breakup of the Roman Empire. He then reminded the delegates they were fundamentally different because Spanish Americans were neither Europeans nor Indians but a hybrid people. They had revolted against Spain and at the same time struggled with indigenous people for control of the land. Their condition was worse than slavery, their task more demanding than the perfection of government because they must exorcize an insidious and debilitating past. Venezuelans were victims: they loved their country but hated the laws governing them because their Spanish rulers had deliberately denied Venezuelans any meaningful participation in their governance. Their only salvation from this misery lay in saving the republic from chaos by forging unity. "The blood of our citizens is varied," he explained; "let it be mixed for the sake of unity. Our Constitution has divided the powers of government: let them be bound together to secure unity." There could be no reformation of the "monstrous edifice" of the laws they had inherited, so they must create a new "temple of Justice" to write new laws suitable to their conditions. If necessary, they could look to the "admirable models" offered by Britain, France, and the United States.[15]

Critics of Bolívar have correctly pointed out the difficulty in looking upon these very disparate models as something that might be used as patchwork solutions until through experience and determination those who governed prepared the people for something better. The speech was analytical, angry, inspirational, sentimental, and more, delivered by a man who could be optimist, seducer, and doubter, a leader who declared that Venezuelans—and, by implication, all Spanish Americans—were victims of a debilitating Spanish rule. Yet Bolívar offered them no reassuring guide for how to confront the infuriating and bewildering questions raised by his denunciation of slavery and his belief that unity rested on acceptance of miscegenated peoples in the revolutionary cause. They must rid themselves of slavery, but who would do the work? They could not win the victory without arming the slaves and people of color, but would the Creoles be able to draw a color line once the shooting stopped? As the Spanish had already discovered, armed slaves incorporated into royalist guerrilla forces had demonstrated through words and behavior that they were unwilling to tolerate older social forms of servitude and deference. Would they proclaim that neither color nor parentage should matter in the new republican social order?

Such were the uncertainties and apprehensions that no one—not even the articulate and persuasive Bolívar—could have assuaged among these delegates whose task seemed far more formidable than that confronting those who had gathered at Philadelphia in 1787. Bolívar sensed their predicament because he had already expressed his views on the conundrum of race. In their 1805 constitution Haitians had dealt with this issue by affirming that every Haitian citizen, whether black, colored, or white, would be considered a "Black." Clearly, that was no option; neither was the U.S. solution as defined by the purpose of the American Colonization Society. In one of his more despondent moments, Bolívar wrote that Spanish Americans were the "abominable product of those predatory tigers who came to America to shed its blood and to interbreed with their victims . . . [and] afterward mixing the dubious fruit of such unions with the offspring of slaves uprooted from Africa." Old-line Federalists sometimes used similar analogies as an example of the implied danger of this racial legacy during the debate over the admission of Missouri as a slave state in 1820. "Among the individuals of a society thus composed," noted a writer in the prestigious *North American Review*, "no feeling of respect, no permanent union of strength for common defence and support can exist, [because] harmony and strength [require] a free and unmingled race of men."[16]

Some of his North American critics had drawn a color line and felt neither moral nor intellectual guilt about the decision. The issue had surfaced during discussion over the admission of Louisiana as a state in 1811–1812 and, more virulently, in the debates over Missouri statehood in 1820–1821. Indeed, the Missouri Compromise, which excluded slavery in newly acquired territories north of 36 degrees, 30 minutes latitude—excepting Missouri, of course—had passed only when the supporters accepted a clause prohibiting entry of free blacks and mulattoes into Missouri. (From that moment, Jefferson wrote, the survival of the union was imperiled.) In both cases, the security of the citizenry depended on the state militias to put down slave rebellions or Indian uprisings, and by implication guarantee white supremacy. The United States may have avoided the militarization of society during its revolution but the early republic did not.

What was the option for an independent Spanish America? Bolívar, frankly, was unsure. In his acceptance of the reality of miscegenation, Bolívar would be a more accommodating participant in modern-day debates about inclusivity and diversity. His decision to arm the slaves, of course, was more problematical for North Americans. In the American Revolution, when the British Crown promised freedom to slaves who would help His Majesty's officers to quell the rebellion, George Washington had solemnly noted that the side arming the Negroes would win the war. Though slaves fought on both sides, neither Washington nor his British adversaries made the arming of slaves a major issue. Early in the Venezuelan war, the Spanish did make the arming of slaves and pardos an integral part of their counterinsurgency campaign. Bolívar, reluctantly but necessarily, ultimately had to follow a similar strategy. Failure to conscript slaves into the patriot army, he believed, would mean that the free population would die in the war and the slaves would survive. The Haitian Revolution had demonstrated that the slaves, if given the opportunity, would kill their masters.[17]

Those slaves who were either conscripted or joined in order to gain their freedom (*libertos*) looked at the war from a very different perspective, as did the slave owners. The conflict and the devastation of the plantation system provided them with an unprecedented opportunity. Some ran away, but such a choice proved risky. They had some assurance that their future would be better, of course. But as the fighting wore on, and patriot commanders had to rely more and more on conscription to replenish their ranks, the resistance of slave owners to relinquishing their laborers for military service heightened. Slaves proved more ambiguous in their reaction. In the early years of the struggle, their willingness to join, particularly in Buenos Aires and Chile, was evident. But the physical hardships of service exacted a devastating toll on their numbers. In his first crossing of the Andes in 1817, half of San Martín's troops in the Army of the Andes were libertos. Six years later, following his campaigns in Chile, Peru, and Ecuador, fewer than 200 returned with him to Argentina. After Angostura, 5,000 slaves joined Bolívar's army for the liberation of New Granada and the invasion of Ecuador. Throughout, their motives for either joining up or resisting conscription were neither uniform nor unambiguous, but those who did serve understood what their commitment should mean. One veteran liberto, imprisoned because he refused to give his former master a part of his earnings, demanded to know why the slave owner wanted "to enslave me again, when the Fatherland has made me free and given me my rights."[18]

Such were the differences in perception about this controversial issue. Beyond that, undeniably, the message at Angostura constituted a triumph for Bolívar, a rebuke to his enemies as well as a candid statement about the place of independent Spanish America in the transatlantic political order. He was the president. He governed under the power of law. He formed a government with a hereditary senate, a strong executive, a judiciary, and what he described as a "moral power" to enlighten the nation. His modern defenders are often quick to cite the Angostura address as an expression of Bolívar's commitment to representative government. His critics persist in reminding us of his doubts that Venezuelans were capable of digesting the liberties and freedoms he extolled. Bolívar always believed he had won a personal victory. He had vanquished his enemies, he wrote a few years later, reminiscing about the importance of what he had achieved. "I left all my opponents buried behind me in the Congress of Angostura."[19]

He departed Angostura elated over the approval and recognition he had received. In summer 1819 he set out on an arduous campaign to lead 2,100 llaneros, New Granadans, and European legionnaires in a march across the Casanare plains and then ever upward into the Andes for the retaking of New Granada. At 13,000 feet, the physical and emotional toll exacted on men, women, and animals became virtually unbearable. A fourth of the battle-hardened Napoleonic war veterans perished on this journey—some to exposure, others to a form of fatigue that comes from sensing too late that they had no earthly reason for being so far from home. Still others became so overpowered with hunger that they were on the verge of cannibalizing the dead until Bolívar permitted the slaughtering of animals for food. On the way down from the mountains, he replenished this army by conscripting men and supplies from local villages.

With these troops, he won a decisive victory at Boyacá on August 7, and three days later triumphantly entered Bogotá.

The campaign was a turning point, both for the man and the army he led. At that moment, he believed victory was inevitable, not because his army fought the just war but because his troops had survived such an arduous journey. And they would go forward because they did not want to go back over that mountain. His followers were neither ideologues nor philosophers nor clerics but shabbily clad fifteen-year-olds who looked twice their age and who subsisted on dried corn, fruit, or animal flesh and followed officers with uniforms made out of blankets with cut-out holes for their heads. They fought with a ferocity that dismayed some of the most hardened British legionnaires. In battle they lacked compassion. They killed their prisoners and stripped the bodies. Yet for every story about their alleged depravity there would be more hideous accounts about Spanish atrocities. An Englishman serving in the Colombian navy intercepted one of Morillo's letters to Ferdinand, in which the Spanish commander described his pacification of Santafé de Bogotá: "Every person, of either sex, who was capable of reading and writing, was put to death. By this cutting off all who were educated, I hoped to effectively arrest the spirit of revolution."[20]

Undeniably, the victory at Boyacá was a turning point in the war, whatever hardships the patriots continued to endure. In the aftermath, Spanish deserters began joining Bolívar's army in increasing numbers. More and more his Spanish adversaries began to suffer from the emotional and physical toll of fighting a guerrilla war. Morillo's troops were now the ones who wore tattered uniforms, went barefoot, subsisted on unsalted beef, festered in unsanitary hospitals, and quartered in hovels. True, Morillo still held Caracas, but Bolívar now had the advantage of the attacker. In fall 1819, he named Santander as vice president of New Granada and set out for his Venezuelan homeland. A few months later, the Congress of Angostura approved several of his more ambitious political proposals, including a declaration of the union of Venezuela with New Granada.[21]

Early in the new year came another blow to the royalists. In Cádiz, the decision of the Spanish Crown to launch another expeditionary force against the Spanish-American rebels precipitated a revolt by a band of officers led by Major Rafael de Riego. They demanded the restoration of the liberal constitution of 1812. When Morillo got word of what had happened, he declared for the constitution and called for a meeting with Bolívar. When they at last met near Trujillo, the Spaniard was taken aback. The enemy who had fought him so fiercely turned out to be a short man wearing a frock coat and riding into camp on a mule. After they had begun to talk, Morillo mellowed under the legendary Bolivarian charm. As if they were two gentlemen who had abruptly called off a duel, they concluded a six-month armistice and, perhaps more significantly, a treaty establishing rules for exchange of prisoners and more humane treatment of civilians. Symbolically if not actually, the meeting made Bolívar the equal of Morillo and conveyed tacit Spanish acceptance of the de facto autonomy of Colombia, the goal of a majority of rebellious Creoles in 1810. But the encounter and the Spanish concessions did not bring closure to the fratricidal passions unleashed in the civil war that had accompanied the decade-old rebellion. Morillo had led an army of pacification into the teeth of that war. Now, in perhaps ways Bolívar never expected, the charge of pacifying a continent lay with the Creoles.[22]

More than at any time, Bolívar now sensed the true cost of the patriot cause. The War to the Death decree he believed so vital several years before had led to the mobilization of slave and pardo troops—men and women who could stake a claim on the postrevolutionary order. They could impose their own demands in the name of defending the patriot faith. This became clear to Bolívar when a defiant Spanish officer violated the truce and renewed the fighting in Venezuela. To defeat the royalist threat and safeguard Venezuelan independence, Bolívar had to rely on Páez's llanero warriors to win a decisive battle at Carabobo (June 24, 1821). A short time later, the Liberator triumphantly entered Caracas and named a new president.

But the real power lay with Páez, who depended on a coterie of officers demanding rewards for their services. In the end, Bolívar chose not to confront the defiant Venezuelans but pacify them with generous land grants and the expedient division of authority throughout the country. In the national assembly in Bogotá, some called for an end to military privilege and even a denial of the vote to soldiers. As O'Leary astutely noted, for its survival the government depended on "the power and influence of the caudillos who had made independence [possible]. Institutions by themselves had no force at all."[23]

These were harsh words, for they expressed a political reality that Bolívar dared not ignore. Still, the political creativity of a new generation continued against the stark background of persistent royalist domination of much of northern South America. In mid-1821, a gathering of patriot representatives met at Cúcuta to ratify the union of Colombia their predecessors at Angostura had drafted. They could not decide on the character of the union—centralist, which Bolívar and the Venezuelans favored; or federalist, the preference of New Granadans who had grown increasingly alarmed about domination by the Venezuelan soldiers. In a shrewd tactical move, Santander chose the centralist camp. In the end, the Cúcuta convention embraced more of the centralist tenets Bolívar personally favored and at least expressed a partial acknowledgment of his 1816 abolition decree by accepting the rule of free birth, which meant that a child of a slave woman would be born free. Slavery survived, however, and even those children born free had to labor until age eighteen for their mother's masters. The convention also eliminated the old colonial sales tax (the despised *alcabala*) as well as Indian tribute and even made tentative gestures in favor of religious tolerance.

Some of these measures Bolívar considered impractical and in fact detrimental to the more pressing needs of national consolidation and order. At times, he despaired over the choices being made by these lawmakers. "Does it not seem to you," he wrote to Santander, "that these legislators, who are more ignorant than evil and more presumptuous than ambitious, will lead us into anarchy and tyranny and finally to destruction?" He followed with another somber judgment: "If it is not the Llaneros who will bring about our ruin, then it will be the gentle philosophers of Colombia."[24]

With these words he voiced some of his innermost fears and doubts about what lay ahead. At the same time, he was implicitly acknowledging that he did not comprehend which of the two would do more damage to the social order. Had he remained a rebel, in thought as well as in deed, he might have made a pact with the royalists, as Iturbide did in Mexico and Thomas

Jefferson recommended. But a revolutionary is different from a rebel. The rebel, if not defeated on the battlefield, may be willing to accept a truce under certain conditions, particularly a grant of autonomy and the implied recognition of equality. Revolutionaries behave differently because they think differently. Although the typologies may be varied, the revolutionary is much more apt to reject any accommodation with his former enemy because he fears the reversal of history more than defeat. As Bolívar had informed Páez, exhausting the enemy was not enough.

Those were the acknowledged credos of the Liberator, yet doubts always intruded in his analyses. The truth of the matter, as he saw it, lay in the fact that the constitution did not fully address the social context of the republic. He disdained the thought of the soldier in power, yet he grieved for the suffering and self-abnegation of those in arms. As he explained to Pedro Gual, "You gentlemen cannot form a true picture of the spirit with which our soldiers are imbued. These are not the soldiers you know; these are soldiers you have never known. . . . They are without hope of gathering the fruit of what they have *won by the lance*. . . . You can be sure, Gual, that we are over an abyss, or, rather, over a volcano, that is about to erupt."[25]

He admired them. He needed them. He felt sorry for them. But when all was said and done he feared their power and their wrath.

The March Southward

There was too little time to dwell on such matters now. More and more, Bolívar was preoccupied with Peru. The word he often invoked to describe what might be in store for Venezuela was *pardocracia*—rule by people of color. The mark of colonial Peru, contrastingly, was *albocracia*—the domination of more than 1.5 million Indians and castas by 140,000 whites. Peru was a mountainous Incan kingdom where Creole and Spaniard were bound not by ideology but by color. Here the Creoles had learned only too well the dangers of pushing too rapidly for a mitigation of the miserable condition of Peru's Indians. In 1809, in Upper Peru (modern Bolivia) rebel Creoles had launched a rebellion against the royalist regime. In their anticipation of a new social order they had welcomed Indian and mestizo to their cause. The Spanish brutally suppressed the movement.

Three years later, with yet another combined Indian-mestizo alliance, the Creoles rose again. For a second time, they met fierce resistance, but in their brief offensive strike they laid siege to La Paz, Puno, and Arequipa. When the marauding force struck La Paz, the Creole officers lost control, and their undisciplined followers commenced a slaughter of the defending garrison and began destroying Spanish property. Their victory was short-lived, and in a three-year retaliatory campaign the royalists were merciless. Whatever unity the Creoles had forged with Indian and mestizo collapsed, and by 1815, as the Spanish counterrevolution swept over the continent, Peru's Creoles conceded that their survival depended on acquiescence to royalist rule, and even that offered little reassurance. Bolívar had astutely identified their dilemma in 1815: "Peru . . . without doubt suffers the greatest subjection and is obliged to make the most sacrifices for the royal cause," he wrote in the famous Jamaica Letter, "[but] the fact remains that it is not tranquil, nor is it capable of restraining the torrent that threatens most of its provinces."[26]

Instinctively, he believed that only he or one of his chosen officers was capable of containing and then directing the force of that torrent. Worse, he confronted other obstacles. He must lead an army through regions of Colombia still fiercely antagonistic to the patriot cause. And then he must bring some order to the beleaguered province of Quito, where only the coastal city of Guayaquil had gained independence. Perhaps his most formidable challenge was another patriot leader, the Argentine José de San Martín, a man by virtually every measure his equal as commander and certainly just as successful. At a moment of disillusion among many of those who had led the Buenos Aires revolution—the only continental uprising that the Spanish had not crushed in the 1814–1816 counterrevolution—San Martín had mobilized an army of Creole, mestizo, colored, and black troops and led them across the Andes to liberate Chile. And he had undertaken this herculean challenge in defiance of his superiors' orders to crush a separatist movement led by José Artigas in the Banda Oriental (modern Uruguay).

That was only the beginning. When San Martín finished the Chilean campaign, he drew on the assistance of a British admiral, Lord Cochrane, and launched an even more impressive assault on coastal Peru. On the eve of victory, however, the Argentine commander chose not to wage the kind of war Bolívar had adopted. San Martín resolved that Peru should be liberated by Peruvians. Truthfully, he feared plunging the country into the anarchy and bloodshed that had swept the Río de la Plata a year before. He discovered too late that his hesitation served only to heighten uncertainties. The Spanish viceroy chose to flee Lima. Fearful of widespread social disorder, the bewildered Creoles responded by accepting San Martín's declaration of independence (July 28, 1821) and granting him supreme authority. They chose him not because they believed in the revolution he espoused but because they seemingly had no alternative. They were happy when he approved the confiscation of Spanish property; sullen over his ending of Indian tribute and acceptance of the free-birth declaration for children of slave mothers.

In truth, San Martín was a chess player weary of the game. Lima was the last post of a thirty-year military career. He had fought for Spain and for Buenos Aires and proved himself the good soldier until he got an order that in his mind no truly good soldier would obey. None of that mattered now. Buenos Aires had disowned him and Lima did not like him. They derisively called him King José, but his authority extended largely to the city and along the coast. In the interior, another movement had erupted among vagrants, bandits, and Indians with old scores to settle. These *montoneros* had no continental strategy. Their passions, hatreds, and commitments were local. Little wonder then, that Lima's Creoles were so apprehensive about their future. A British officer who witnessed these events wrote that Lima's Creoles were terrified "that the slave population of the city meant to take advantage of the absence of the [royalist] troops, to rise in a body and massacre the whites." They feared also the armed Indians under San Martín's command, believing them to be "savage and undisciplined."[27]

Venezuelan and New Granadan Creoles had expressed similar fears about pardo and black soldiers, but their white colleagues in Lima confronted something more ominous—the numbers of Indians among them and the apprehension that these were people not only with old grievances but with the memory of their ancestral heritage of an Incan kingdom. Independence would do little to address the first and nothing to restore the second. Bolívar was unsympathetic to San Martín's predicament. And he was not going to be outdone or upstaged by his Argentine counterpart. He, not San Martín, was the chosen son of the patriot cause.

At the moment, however, Bolívar was confronted with the onerous task of pacifying Pasto, a region of Colombia that Santander had once called "the graveyard of the brave." For a time, Bolívar considered a march to the coast, then a sea voyage to Guayaquil. There he planned to join his forces with those of one of his ablest officers, José Antonio de Sucre, who commanded a thousand-man army in the city. But the plan had to be abandoned when in early 1822 Bolívar got word that a royalist force had landed on Ecuador's north coast and had begun a march inland toward Quito.

Bolívar now had the less glorious and to him more difficult challenge of subduing Pasto while Sucre maneuvered his Colombian soldiers for a strike against Quito. On the evening of May 22, 1822, Sucre stationed his troops on the southern slopes of Mount Pichincha, the massive volcano on the city's outskirts. At eight the next morning, the royalist commander unwisely sent his defenders on a laborious and enervating ninety-minute climb to do battle. By noon, the rested patriots had won a stupendous victory. Within a few days, the last Spanish ruler of Ecuador had left the country. Ecuador had been liberated, but not by the Liberator. Six weeks earlier, Pasto's royalists had fought Bolívar to a standstill at Bomb005á, a battle that had cost him one-third of his troops. Only reinforcements hastily sent to him by Santander enabled him to overcome the enemy and take Pasto. News about the fall of Quito did not noticeably raise his spirits, however. As others were touting Sucre's victory, Bolívar scribbled his assessment in one of his many letters to Santander: "Sucre had a larger number of troops and a smaller number of enemies than I, [but] we, on the other hand, found ourselves in a veritable hell and fought with the Devil."[28]

In time, he reconciled with Sucre, who continued to perform superbly and with Bolívar's endorsement became Bolivia's first president. And it was Sucre who made possible the Liberator's triumphant entry into Quito, where he basked in the joyous outburst of cries of "Viva Bolívar" and "Viva nuestro Libertador" from a people who reputedly hated the Spaniards and adored the Colombians. There he met the last woman in his life who mattered to him—Manuela Sáenz del Thorne, the illegitimate daughter of a Spaniard. Her life had been almost as tumultuous as Bolívar's. At an early age, her father had sent her to a convent but she was expelled when the mother superior discovered she had an affair with a Spanish officer. Her personal life scandalized proper society. She liked to play cards. She smoked cigars. She could ride a horse as well as any man. In 1817, she had married a well-off middle-aged British merchant, who took her to Lima.

She moved easily in *limeño* society and clandestinely served the patriot cause. Not surprisingly, Bolívar found this woman captivating, different in almost every respect from the succession of mistresses he had known since the untimely death of his wife. In their first encounter, at a ball given in his honor, she was polite but instinctively distanced herself from him. Few women snubbed him, and, not to be denied, he pursued her. They spent twelve amorous nights together, the passionate inaugural of a relationship that would last for another eight years. Their encounter, wrote one of Bolívar's most perceptive biographers, was the "decisive moment of her existence."[29]

Manuela provided Bolívar with essential information about San Martín before their famous meeting (July 26 and 27, 1822)—stories about the Argentine's recurrent illness, his caution in the taking of Lima, the deplorable condition of his troops, and, perhaps most damaging, the reasons why Lord Cochrane and most of the Argentine officers had deserted his command. San Martín had reckoned that with an early arrival in Guayaquil he would be able to woo the city into the Peruvian orbit. What occurred proved to be a disappointment, for Bolívar beat him to the city by two weeks, and when San Martín finally disembarked he soon learned that the combination of

Bolivarian charm and politicking had converted Guayaquil's citizenry into avid supporters of Colombia.

The conversations between the two men, held behind closed doors, lasted less than two days, and the details have been clouded in controversy ever since. What we do know is that Bolívar was tentative in his commitment of assistance in the Peruvian situation and, true to character, unwilling to serve under San Martín. Contrastingly, San Martín may have uttered an equally vague pledge to follow Bolívar's lead, though it must have been clear to both that such an arrangement could never have worked. San Martín came from modest circumstances, but he did not share Bolívar's risky strategy of raising the expectations of slaves and pardos about their future if they fought for the patriot cause. His brief Peruvian experience had taught him a social lesson: the Creole aristocracy and the Lima merchant classes had to unite to combat the revolutionaries in the mountains. In Peru he had acquiesced to the slave owners' demands not to conscript their slaves for military service. The "barriers that separated the different classes of people had to be maintained in order to maintain the rule of the educated."[30]

Both men commanded black and pardo troops and shared a continental vision, but they had little else in common. Put simply, they were of such different temperaments and experience that they could never have formed a military bond. San Martín was a general in the Spanish tradition and a monarchist and of the British variety that Bolívar professed to admire, but these were ephemeral similarities. Bolívar was the quintessential guerrilla who had made himself over into the continental strategist, self-taught and inspired. San Martín wanted to liberate Spanish America without severing the traditional relationship between social classes. He was frankly fearful of the social chaos that might consume the continent, which explains his reverence for monarchical traditions. For Bolívar, the age of monarchy had passed, but, unlike San Martín, the Venezuelan had not yet fully absorbed the logic that if you remove the king as head or father you must symbolically replace him. San Martín's strategy may have offered the less painful and certainly the less destructive outcomes, but after his meeting with Bolívar this chess-playing Argentine knew he had been checkmated.[31]

He had received the "Bolívar treatment." Less than two months later (on September 22, 1822), San Martín resigned his Peruvian command, warning the stupefied legislators of the dangers of military rule. Shortly, he left for Chile and, ultimately, went into exile. In his absence, the country collapsed into anarchy, with a Spanish army in the south and rival patriot forces in the north. In these conditions, Lima's frustrated Creoles had no alternative but to appeal to Bolívar to rescue them from anarchy. Flush with a succession of victories both professional and personal, Bolívar acknowledged their predicament and committed himself to resolving the fratricidal conflicts in what he described as the Peruvian cauldron.

Truly, he was the Liberator.

CHAPTER FIVE

~

The Victor

By mid-1822, as Bolívar prepared his strategy for the Peruvian campaign, the European powers that might otherwise have abetted the royalist cause had already resolved that the western question—the Spanish-American independence movement—would not become a matter requiring an international meeting, as had the eastern question and the uprising against Ottoman rule by the Greeks. The rebellion within the Spanish empire was less unsettling to the fragile international system than the French Revolution, nor had the restored Spanish monarchy proved capable of mobilizing European allies on its behalf.

As Bolívar had predicted, the British had made sure of that, and the French and Russian governments had demonstrated that they were more interested in opening up trade with a Spanish-American market than in propping up Ferdinand VII's faltering authority. A succession of patriot victories, commencing with Bolívar's triumph at Boyocá in 1819, the impact of the Riego revolt on royalist morale in 1820, and the abrupt decision of the United States to recognize Colombian independence in 1822 appeared to confirm an inevitable patriot triumph. In the abbreviated span of six years, even the once doubtful John Quincy Adams would conclude that Colombian independence signified that "the colonial domination of Europe over the American hemisphere has fallen, and is crumbling into dust."[1]

Bolívar's assessment of what lay ahead for the patriot cause was not so reassuring. In the Jamaica Letter of September 1815, he had described Peru as a corrupt society with a white aristocracy stubbornly opposed to democracy and a mass of Indians, pardos, and freed slaves just as resolutely rejecting their domination.

The Peruvian Quagmire

Nothing he had experienced in his previous campaigns adequately prepared Bolívar for what he faced in Peru. As a military leader, he had adapted to the experience of mobilizing slave and pardo soldiers, but he had yet to encounter such large numbers of indigenous peoples, and their loyalty and commitment remained suspect, regardless of the cause they served. Until the arrival of San Martín, both sides had exploited them as bearers of arms or auxiliaries. Soldiers, republican and royalist, destroyed their crops and stole their animals and chickens. They had little expectation that a patriot victory would bring much improvement or change in their lives.

Peru in 1823 remained two societies—the "republic of Indians," outwardly submissive but with its numbers ominously threatening, and the "republic of Spaniards," those of European and American birth as well as mestizos and Afro-Peruvians. In Venezuela, New Granada, and Ecuador, Bolívar had been able to mobilize those Creoles who felt alienated from a debilitated and weakened Spanish crown. There was no comparable unifying spirit among Peru's Creole elite, as San Martín had sadly discovered, so Bolívar resolved to bring about a radical change in the nation's political culture.[2]

San Martín lacked the Liberator's arrogance. Bolívar persuaded himself that his invitation to enter the country reflected a genuine commitment by Peruvian Creoles to the patriot cause. And his grand reception when he rode into Lima (September 1, 1823) appeared to confirm that belief. A throng of Peruvian, Chilean, and Argentine troops and local dignitaries cheered him as he rode triumphantly into the city. Not since his arrival in Caracas after the Admirable Campaign had he received such a stupendous welcome. An Englishman who witnessed the event alertly noted the Liberator's bearing: "He is a small thin man. . . . [H]is face is well formed but wrinkled by fatigue and weariness, [yet] he has a fire in his eyes. . . . Never have I seen a face that expresses a more exact description of a man."[3]

In his private moments, the man with fire in his eyes referred to Peru as a "chamber of horrors." His aide-de-camp Daniel O'Leary described the country as a corpse. There were four patriot armies, a royalist army, and two presidents, one of whom continually intrigued with the royalists while the other embezzled the national treasury. In similar circumstances, San Martín had elected to leave the country. Bolívar chose to accept a dictatorship. His friends warned him that his decision would do nothing but damage his reputation, but he was convinced that to abandon Peru, as San Martín had done, would be tantamount to a betrayal of the patriot cause. In a stroke of Bolivarian realpolitik, he convinced the most obstreperous of the two presidents, José de la Riva Agüero, that continued warring with Congress would mean the "inevitable ruin of Peru."[4]

Bolívar had chosen to stay the course. He had at least two reasons to do so. In the north, one of the alienated ex-presidents commenced negotiating with the Spanish and so roused the enmity of his own troops that they deposed him. This act Bolívar interpreted as a sign that those from below would sustain the revolution. And the political rivalries of the North Atlantic powers, he now believed more strongly than ever, favored the patriots. Four months before embarking for Peru, he had written to Sucre, "It does not suit England's purpose for any European nation, like Spain . . . to retain a colony in America. . . . England . . . desires to form an alliance with all the free peoples of America and Europe . . . in order to place herself at the head of these peoples and rule the world."[5]

Such was his judgment about the national interest of other nations, particularly Great Britain, and at the moment he wrote those words he frankly did not know if his assessment was realistic or just wishful thinking. In any event, he resolved to pacify the Peruvian beast. To the nation's Creoles, he became the Janus-faced presence, a dictator who served as both persecutor and protector. He rebuked the Creoles for their continuing loyalties to the old order and when they rejected his demands he scorned them. Under pressure, they acquiesced, not out of any commitment to the cause he preached but out of self-interest, as they could no longer look to the Crown for protection. He was their savior, or so he believed.

Perhaps instinctively, they understood his purpose in importing the revolution into Peru; only the revolution he bore was not the revolution they wanted. They might accept a Peruvian republic but only if it preserved the royalist social agenda. San Martín, Bolívar's equal as military commander but his inferior as the committed revolutionary, had abandoned the Peruvian Creoles to their own fate. Bolívar resolved to save them by the expedient of destroying any hope that the old social order could be restored. He brought in fresh recruits from Colombia to renew the war and paid for it by seizing royalist property, exacting tribute from the church, and levying new taxes.

With such measures Bolívar brought at least some unity to the patriot cause in Peru—a coercive unity, perhaps, but his measures brought results. In Spain, the liberal resurgence collapsed when a French army restored Ferdinand VII's total authority. But in Peru, the last bastion of mainland overseas Spain, Bolívar triumphed. With the inestimable aid of Sucre, he mobilized a

9,000-man army, marched it ever upward into the Andean highlands, and on August 6, 1824, at a plain called Junín, led them in a cavalry battle in which not one shot was fired. His army was quintessentially American—Argentine gauchos, Chilean peasants, Venezuelan llaneros, Peruvians, Ecuadorians, and libertos. The patriots were abler swordsmen and their lances were longer. Junín was the silent battle. It lasted only ninety minutes. The royalists lost 400 men, the patriots 120, insignificant numbers by European standards, but the victory restored a flagging patriot confidence. "The genius of America led us," Bolívar wrote, "and fortune smiled on us."[6]

Junín was not the final battle, it must be noted. That clash occurred in December 1824 at Ayacucho, where Sucre was in command because the Colombian congress had informed Bolívar that he no longer had the authority to continue the war in Peru. This was not the first time that civilians reminded the Liberator that he was their agent, nor would it be the last. No matter. Ayacucho was the last major stand of royalist Spain in the Americas until the end of the nineteenth century, when a dedicated generation of Cuban revolutionaries unleashed yet another assault against the motherland that ended, sadly, when the island as well as Puerto Rico passed from one ruler to another.

For Bolívar, the victory at Ayacucho proved bittersweet. For nine years he and his coterie of lieutenants had led a patriot struggle in northern Spanish America against more than 25,000 Spanish soldiers and untold and ever-shifting numbers of white, pardo, black, and Indian royalist allies. True, the Spanish invader in the Bolivarian theater of war had lost more than 16,000 troops, a majority from mosquito-borne diseases, poor diet, contaminated water, and the forbidding terrain. Through trials and setbacks, Bolívar and his comrades had adapted to what a U.S. confidential agent had described as a struggle of such "savage barbarities and oppressions" that a respect for public sensibility dictated that later generations should be spared reading about the details. A British observer seconded his somber assessment in commenting about post-Ayacucho Peru: Much of the wealth, he wrote, disappeared, some of the booty going to Spain, some to England, and still more taken out in the packs of troops from Buenos Aires, Chile, and Colombia.[7]

In the former viceroyalty of New Granada, the war was particularly devastating—governments bankrupted, cities and towns decimated by the recurring shifts of fortune in the battle between patriot and royalist troops, and horrific losses of population. The Spanish counterrevolution had indeed been defeated, Bolívar wrote a few weeks after the Ayacucho victory, yet he foresaw "civil war and disorder breaking out in all directions and spreading from country to country. I see my native gods consumed by domestic fire."

Sporadic violence and banditry in his native Venezuela, where almost fifteen years of violence and destruction had reduced the population by one-fourth, was particularly disheartening. The fractured independent nations of Spanish America had only one choice to survive and, just as important, to assume their rightful place in the family of modern nations—to craft a federation, "a temple of sanctuary from criminal trends."[8]

He had replaced the Spaniard Morillo as the leader of an army of pacification. In triumph, Bolívar confronted a potentially more dangerous enemy: dozens of Creole leaders who for personal as well as political reasons could not afford to permit him to exercise the power in peacetime that he had assumed in the course of the war. But he had struggled for fifteen years to attain this victory, and he had no intention of giving up the power and glory he believed he had earned without a fight.

The Continental Vision

The Ayacucho capitulation meant more than a military triumph. Symbolically, if not legally, Spain and America were reunited. In that respect, perhaps, the settlement with the motherland bore a reassuring similarity to that crafted three years earlier in Mexico, when the Pact of Iguala had guaranteed equality between Spaniard and Creole, independence, and protection of the Catholic religion. Further, Iguala had enabled the Creole Agustín de Iturbide (who was the same age as Bolívar) to assume a Mexican throne as Agustín I. As a royalist officer, Iturbide had waged a merciless war against Mexican insurgents and the social revolution their cause represented. His imperial rule, Bolívar noted sarcastically, depended on the "grace of God and of bayonets." Bereft of money and political support, Agustín I abdicated in March 1823, fled to exile in England, then a year later tried to return to power. Two days after his landing, he was captured and shot.

Bolívar often referred to the Mexican experience and the repudiation and death of Iturbide as an example of the futility of creating another monarchy in Spanish America. And he remained alert to the possibility of another assault from abroad. His immediate goal, then, was the convening of a special congress to create a defensive league of former Spanish colonies, a plan he had initially outlined in the 1815 Jamaica Letter and, later, in correspondence with patriot leaders in Peru, Buenos Aires, and Chile. The federation he had in mind offered not a substitute for the national governments that had sprung up over the past half dozen years but a means of preserving the nascent republics and at the same time a formal structure to secure both internal and external peace. He was particularly concerned about unrest in his native Venezuela, where his old comrades were often at loggerheads with what they considered the high-handed ways of vice president Santander in Bogotá. Rightly or wrongly, Bolívar considered their protests as the first step toward anarchy, and the only way to deal with the crisis lay in a continental federation. In an implied threat to abandon the entire project, he averred to Santander that "only [the] hope that the American congress will meet, keeps me in America."[9]

It is difficult to invoke Bolívar's often diffuse and even contradictory statements about Spanish-American unity and come up with a precise understanding of what he had in mind for this congress. Certainly, he was more the continentalist than nationalist, and his sense of identity as American gradually supplanted the one he felt for his native Venezuela. "Americans," he wrote in 1818, "should have but a single *patria* [homeland]." Within three years, he discarded this romantic notion in favor of a strong federation of five states, a potential colossus that would astonish European governments and take its place in the international community of nations. Deeply troubled by the dissonant voices within the patriot ranks, he viewed the federation as a supranational device for controlling "diabolic extremes"—a veiled reference to dissidents in Venezuela and in the Río de la Plata—among the federated states, which he now referred to as "sisters," not "nations."[10]

The invitations went out a few days before the Ayacucho victory to the governments of Mexico, the Central American federation, Chile, Río de la Plata (Argentina), and Colombia, with the delegates scheduled to meet in Panama City in 1826. Viewed from a historical perspective, Bolívar's outline is often offered up as a brilliant initial design for the later Pan American Union and the modern Organization of American States. In actuality, however, he had a narrower conception for continental unity, excluding Haiti, Brazil, and, most controversially, the United States, an omission many have cited as evidence of the Liberator's suspicions about the domineering and interventionist U.S. role in the hemisphere from the era of Jefferson to the present. Bolívar was never so devious. He believed that the North American republic was too different—both in the character of its people and its government—to be included.

Haiti, frankly, offered an even more striking disparity in customs and its frightening reminder as a source of slave rebellion and racial equality. Bolívar was committed to the abolition of slavery and, by nineteenth-century standards, racial equality, but he recognized that neither could be achieved as immediate goals without imperiling his strategy for achieving unity among the new republics. To fight a war using the argument that black slaves and pardos must be enlisted in the struggle for victory was a tactic that might make sense to a Creole slaveholder, but that same person might demur at granting equality to them. From this perspective, Bolívar's thinking was not that different from Abraham Lincoln's tormented personal debate over how to preserve the union. And, like Lincoln, through the ordeal of war and the choices he had made to fight that war, Bolívar had gradually but perceptibly altered the social and racial agenda of his white Creole inheritance. The Congress of Panama, he was now firmly convinced, would enact measures that would not only preserve internal order in the federated states but, more important, would diminish the debilitating social legacies of birth and color, thus enabling his America to avoid the horrors of another Haitian revolution and no longer fear the "numerical preponderance of [the continent's] primitive inhabitants."[11]

But the gravamen of the case was his estimation of Great Britain and British interests in the new republic. Great Britain, he believed, would not only extend diplomatic recognition to the new republics but with its investments and commerce protect them. He was reluctant to include Brazil because its government was a monarchy. Brazil and the United States did receive invitations, largely because Santander and the Central American federation favored the idea. And to Bolívar's delight the British dispatched an observer.

Two issues about Bolívar's plan for a Spanish-American federation continue to spark controversy and, occasionally, acrimonious debate—the posture of U.S. leaders toward the plan and, second, the import and legacy of what was ultimately achieved.

Briefly, the traditional accounts of the international history of the Western hemisphere in the 1820s identify twin U.S. goals, both expressed in President James Monroe's December 1823 message to Congress. The first was a statement of opposition to any efforts by the so-called Holy Alliance of European powers not only to crush the Greek rebellion but to assist Spain in a recovery of its New World colonies—the noncolonization principle—and a belief in the future of republican government in Spanish America. (North American policy toward the Caribbean, understandably, hinged on apprehensions about growing British influence in Spanish Cuba, continuing fears of slave rebellion, the creation of "another Haiti," and the indirect but nonetheless tangible links between the Haitian revolution and slave revolts in the United States.) By the mid-1820s, John Quincy Adams, now president, had softened his earlier views about identifying the United States with the Spanish-American cause. So, too, had the once-visceral editorialists of the *North American Review*. "The time has come," wrote one contributor, "when the most skeptical are obliged to lay aside their doubts; South America is free; her independence is as completely established as was that of our own states at any time between the declaration of independence and the establishment of peace."[12]

The mood in the Congress, however, had changed since Henry Clay (now secretary of state) had delivered his passionate appeals for recognition of the new republics. Recognition was no longer a central issue; the universality or particularity of Monroe's message was. In the congressional discussions about whether or not the Congress should formally endorse what the president recommended, the "Hellenic bloc" led by Daniel Webster lost out in its verbal battle to invoke Monroe's principles not only in Spanish America but presumably with equal vigor in defense of the Greek cause. "I think we have as much in community with the Greeks as with the inhabitants of the Andes," Webster wrote to Edward Everett, editor of the *North American Review*, and declared to his colleagues that if the United States (and England) did not stand up to the menace of the Holy Alliance in both Greece and Spanish America, then "it will be resisted nowhere. If there is no vigor in the Saxon race to withstand it, there is not to be looked for elsewhere."[13]

Webster missed the point. What North Americans had in common with the Greeks was a philosophy. What they shared with Bolívar was alienation from and fear of Europe and, more than that, a lasting ambivalence about slavery and people of color in the republican order. In victory the "Americanists" did not push for a formal endorsement of what Monroe had stated, and, as Bolívar correctly sensed, the United States had again shown its Janus-face to its southern neighbors: its commitment to a hemispheric bond was qualified. When the invitation for a U.S. delegation to the Congress of Panama finally arrived, the Congress became mired in debate over the mission and the implications of an "entangling alliance" (though President Washington had France in mind when he wrote those words) or participation in any conference where antislavery resolutions might be put forward or, worse, where black or colored delegates would participate. Throughout the discussions the commingled issues of the Haitian revolution, the dangers of slave insurrection in the United States, and the role of black and mulatto in the new states of Spanish America surfaced repeatedly. Senator Thomas Hart Benton of Missouri put the matter bluntly and succinctly when he warned about dispatching any U.S. delegates to a conference in which antislavery legislation might be discussed or to treat with governments "who have already put the black man upon an equality with the white, not only in their constitutions but in real life . . . [or] who have . . . black generals in their armies and mulatto senators in their congresses!"[14]

In the end, the mission was approved, but one of the commissioners died en route, and the second arrived after the conferees had fled the pestilential Panamanian venue for the much more agreeable climate of Tacubaya, Mexico.

If we set aside the misplaced and largely undeserved praise about the Congress of Panama as a forerunner of the inter-American system, then its apparent significance for understanding the Bolivarian legacy lies principally in its ambitious project for a defensive alliance and its implied call for Spanish-American unity. When the conference met, however, three independent states (Argentina, Brazil, and Chile) had no representation. None of the acts passed by the four attending delegations from Peru, Colombia, Central America, and Mexico gained effect. But the four states that were represented eventually divided into twelve independent nations, and the lukewarm reaction of the United States and the parallel skills of the British representative virtually ensured that Britain would exercise greater influence in nineteenth-century Latin America than the United States.[15]

But there is another, too little appreciated link between the Spanish-American cause and, particularly, Bolívar, and those U.S. leaders who expressed a tentative judgment about the prospects for its republican future. As they aged, the first generation of North American revolutionaries believed that the dissolution of the Spanish empire presented them with dilemmas similar to those they had encountered in the breakdown of the British empire. This observed experience, together with the persistent internal political and sectional squabbling generally identified with the rise of political parties, convinced them that both internal and external threats to national unity must be confronted. With the rise of Andrew Jackson, however, the public concerns about the future of the union hinged more and more on internal matters, notably slavery and the division between slave and nonslave states. In the process, the older appeal of "good neighborliness" among the hemispheric republics, north and south, weakened before the democratic urges from below. Monroe's statement, then, was aimed not so much to prevent a European threat to an independent Spanish America—which the nation was virtually powerless to prevent—but to offer a political statement of unilateral resolve to counter Jackson's appeal and, frankly, ensure that John Quincy Adams would become the next president. As for relations with the new republics to the south, the United States, Adams wrote in the aftermath of the Panama fiasco, would seek an amicable but not a strong bond. Good neighborhood had become not a solution but a problem.[16]

Both Latin American and even North American scholars often cite these and other contemporary observations as important indicators of the notably diminishing commitment of the United States to any meaningful identification with the Spanish-American wars of independence and as validation of Bolívar's warnings about the North American peril. In actuality, however, one important source North Americans drew on to make these somber appraisals was Bolívar himself. The contributor to the *North American Review* noted above went on to express doubts "that harmonious and well adjusted governments are to spring up at once from the soil of the South American republics" and invoked Bolívar's comments in the 1819 Angostura address "that the people of America, bound with the triple yoke of ignorance, tyranny, and vice, could not acquire either knowledge, power, or virtue." After receiving intelligence reports about Bolívar's apparent diminished enthusiasm for a Spanish-American federation, Secretary of State Clay scribbled in his instructions to the emissaries to the Congress of Panama that "it is probable that he does not look upon the Congress in the same interesting light that he formerly did. Still the objects . . . are so highly important, that the President thinks their accomplishments ought not to be abandoned whilst any hope remains."[17]

Following the U.S. lead, the British had commenced to recognize the independence of the new republics, and, just as important, a coterie of London bankers had provided desperately needed loans. And, though he persistently denied that he sought such glory, in February 1825 the Peruvian congress, once his nemesis, cast a medal and erected an equestrian statue in his honor. At the same time, the congress granted to him the stupendous honorarium of a million pesos and another million for his army of liberation. The personal grant Bolívar allocated to the improvement of Caracas and other cities in Colombia. And from the heirs of George Washington he received what was to him an unparalleled recognition: a packet containing a gold medallion commemorating the British surrender at Yorktown and a letter signed by the Marquis de Lafayette informing him that the donors considered Bolívar to be the "second Washington of the New World."[18]

The Uncertainties of Victory

In the first year after the Spanish capitulation at Ayacucho, Bolívar experienced virtually all the emotions that are the deserved rewards of the victorious warrior. He enjoyed the affection of Manuela, the admiration of his lieutenants, and a degree of international acclaim that would have been unthinkable only a few years before.

More and more he dwelt on the recurring political and social questions left unresolved by the victory over the royalists and the creation of new republican governments. Inevitably, as North American and Haitian leaders had acknowledged, such questions centered on the nature of power and the place of people of color in the new political order. Put differently, how was it possible for those who had rejected monarchy to retain the real and symbolic authority of a monarch in order to contain the divisive and anarchic forces unleashed by the toppling of the old order? Monarchical societies, to be sure, had social ranks in which parentage and skin color mattered, but how did one measure these complex social realities in a republican society? Informally if not always explicitly, the French had instituted the categories of "active" and "passive" citizenry, but these designations did not neatly fit the political and social patterns of Spanish America.

Bolívar the liberal egalitarian consistently vowed that the new republics should establish legal equality, regardless of color, and abolish slavery, but he often followed with worrisome comments that these measures might not be sufficient to appease those with old grudges against the Creoles. "Legal equality does not satisfy the spirit of the people who want absolute equality . . . and after that a pardocracy . . . and the extermination of the privileged classes," he solemnly observed, adding later, "he who escapes with his white face will be fortunate indeed." Neither the long struggle for independence nor the guarantees of the new constitutions could alter the fundamental thinking of people of color. The only protection for a white minority, then, lay with a despotic ruler, yet when his old comrade Páez, citing the French example, urged him to proclaim himself emperor (as had Napoleon), Bolívar rejected the idea on the grounds "that the coloured population would interpret monarchy as a denial of all their hopes for equality."[19]

We have in these often convoluted and contradictory musings about governance and color further evidence about why several prominent North American leaders altered their initial, sometimes favorable, impressions of Bolívar. To a U.S. naval officer who dined with him in 1824, Bolívar expressed his deepest admiration for George Washington, his disdain for the Spanish who had "mixed with [N]egroes and Indians and devils and have formed the most accursed race that ever lived," and his belief that only immigration from Europe and North America would bring prosperity to Spanish America. The following New Year's Day, Henry Clay (at the time a hopeful claimant to the presidency) toasted Bolívar in absentia as the "second George Washington."

In the course of the year, troubling rumors of a Colombian-Mexican assault on Spanish Cuba and Puerto Rico revived old fears about the Liberator and the kind of war he had waged. News of the power entrusted to Bolívar by the Peruvian congress and the details about the Bolivian constitution reinforced these suspicions about his motives, particularly in the context of the rumored assault against Cuba. Alexander Everett, a confidant of John Quincy Adams and minister to Spain, put the issue succinctly in a January 1827 dispatch: "[T]he [possible] establishment of a military despotism in Colombia and Peru," Everett speculated, would seek "to place an advanced post on the island of Cuba. . . . A military despot of talent and experience at the head of a black army is certainly not the sort of neighbour we should naturally wish . . . to place on our Southern frontier."[20]

By then, Bolívar confronted the more troublesome task of reconciling the fractious bands of patriots who had triumphed in the long war against the royalist but who persisted in battling one another. An early test came in Upper Peru, where a royalist band continued to battle a patriot force Bolívar had entrusted to Sucre. Upper Peru had once formed a part of the Viceroyalty of La Plata. In 1809 its dissidents had launched their own rebellion, and after the continental war exploded, royalists from Peru and patriots from Buenos Aires warred over its future. The porteños emerged victorious, and with an ideological zeal typical of the rebellion in the La Plata region, they declared equality between creoles and the region's Indian majority. In the process, they angered their putative beneficiaries with their disrespect of local religious and social customs. Debate centered on union with Argentina or with Peru.

Bolívar himself astutely concluded that independence would be more acceptable, although he envisioned a semiautonomous province within a larger Andean federation. But Sucre, not Bolívar, directed affairs in Upper Peru, and when a constituent assembly finally convened in Chuquisaca (later renamed Sucre) the delegates voted for independence and sovereignty. They adopted the name of the República Bolívar, which they eventually shortened to Bolivia. When Bolívar crossed into the new republic in September, he was taken aback by the condition of the indigenous population he encountered along the route. He set about reissuing several of the decrees San Martín had refrained from enforcing—abolition of Indian tribute and forced labor—and added some new ones, among them a call for the breakup of Indian communal lands into private tracts. When he at last arrived in Chuquisaca, the national assembly petitioned him to write a new constitution for the republic that bore his name.

The document Bolívar drew up resembled in its purpose if not its language a constitutional monarchy a la bolivariana. It provided for a president with limited power but who served as long as he wished and could name his own successor. (He sometimes observed that the first generation of U.S. presidents had in effect chosen their successors.) With the "Censors"—a variation of the "Moral Power" he had outlined in the Angostura address—he envisioned a third house attached to the archetypal dual legislative branch. To this framework he appended a distinct "Electoral Power," a system of indirect elections and severely limited to literates. Most Bolivians thus stood excluded from the political process. In keeping with the liberal tenets of the age, and his own convictions, he added a clause abolishing slavery and upholding religious tolerance.

The assembly adopted the constitution, although without approving his plea for immediate abolition or religious freedom. Viewed through a historical prism, it provided for a regime that more closely resembled that crafted by Napoleon to undermine the ideals of the French Revolution than one committed to the needs of the Bolivian people. More pointedly, the Bolivian constitution is often identified as yet another indicator of Bolívar's doubts about the capacity of liberated peoples to "digest" the blessings of freedom with the guidance of enlightened leaders and another illustration of his arrogance.

Perhaps. But there are overlooked clues to Bolívar's innermost thoughts and fears in this and other pieces of evidence in his papers. In the initial paragraph of his message to the Bolivian congress, he professed "embarrassment and trepidation" at the request to write a constitution for the new republic. He was a soldier not a solon, he informed them, but they had asked him to write their fundamental law. "I do not know who suffers most," he confessed, "you for the evils that may result from the laws you have asked of me, or I, for the opprobrium to which you have condemned me by your confidence." Entrusted with a task by those who knew him only by his unarguably impressive reputation as a warrior, he offered them a document with a somber warning: "Beware of the sea that you are about to cross in a fragile bark with so inexperienced a pilot at the helm."[21]

The Enemy Within

If Bolívar intended the preamble to his letter as an effort to distract the delegates from his ambitions to direct their lives—if not as another Napoleon then perhaps as a modern Augustus Caesar—they saw right through the charade. If he wished to convey to them, and the legions of political and military allies, friends, and sycophants, that he was too physically and emotionally exhausted to go on, no one would have believed him. Frankly, he rarely comported himself in a modest or self-effacing manner. His determination to clone the Bolivian constitution onto the Peruvian and then the Colombian polities—all of them bound under a magnificent Federation of the Andes with its president-for-life Bolívar at the head—was a signal of his intention to hold onto power. Little wonder that even his friends found him disingenuous when he disdained powers urged upon him yet determinedly opposed anybody who dared try and take them from him. He understood the willingness of some, including onetime allies, to find an alternate path, a government without him at the helm, and not without reason he persuaded himself that he and not they expressed the will of the people.

What he failed to grasp, until it was too late, was that he as revolutionary and liberator may have served more the privileged Creole society he so often condemned and not the cause of Spanish America's vast and amorphous peoples. He had mobilized the castas and slaves in a struggle to restore the Creoles to their former primacy in the social order. Now, at the moment of triumph and despite his warnings of pardocracia, his behavior was unsettling to some of his former allies. Little wonder, then, that in victory some of his former Creole allies looked on him more and more not as the solution but as their biggest problem.

He inspired loyalty, jealousy, and fear, often in the same person. If few understood him, it really was not for want of trying, for his behavior offered few clues to what he was thinking. He was the universalist true believer with a solution for particularist societies, yet when for good reasons the beneficiaries of his designs found his proposals wanting, he could demonstrate a willingness to acknowledge the error. He could adapt, often brilliantly, to the changing tactics of war but not to the vagaries of peacetime. The Bolivian constitution offers an illustration. The document he drafted bore more resemblance to the Roman than the Spanish-American political reality. Even more damaging may have been his decision to turn over the new republic's educational system to his old mentor, Simón Rodríguez, who had spent the previous quarter-century in Europe as a bon vivant among the socialists of Paris, London, and Geneva. In Chuquisaca, Rodríguez became the secular educational priest, dedicated to erasing all distinctions between people of color and educating all in the faith of reason, not custom or tradition. Little wonder that after Bolívar's departure, Sucre kicked Rodríguez out.[22]

In time, Bolívar appeared willing to scrap the Bolivian constitution, but what hurt even more was the defiance of his old comrade from the Venezuelan plains, José Antonio Páez, who for better or worse decided that he must choose between the increasingly controlling reach of vice president Santander in Bogotá or an increasingly restive Venezuelan military. As had others, Páez instinctively looked to his old chief to settle matters. If Bolívar became a monarch, Páez wrote, he could resolve this injustice perpetrated on the Venezuelan nation by a cabal of Granadans. The good leader does not allow the constitution to stand in the way of helping the people. And when authorities in Bogotá demanded that Páez present himself to answer charges of military misconduct, he refused. His fellow officers applauded his bravery.

Though he was privately angry, Bolívar did not reprimand Páez. In early July 1826 when Bolívar wrote to Santander about the Venezuelan affair, he offered not a solution but an analysis. "I want no more civil wars," he confided, and then went so far as to acknowledge that "all is lost if Páez continues upon the path of insurrection." He did not follow with a resolve to crush it but solemnly admitted he was unwilling to carry out "this abominable discretionary power." He then lapsed into a rambling commentary about the inevitable disorder and racial conflict that he foresaw in the future of the new republics. Reform of the laws offered no solution to the looming racial crisis, he believed. "We shall have more and more of Africa," and "anyone with a white skin who escapes will be fortunate."[23]

To be precise, the Páez rebellion was not a racial affair but a challenge by the periphery to the central authority, a form of defiance common to virtually every new nation in the Americas. For a few months in late 1826, Bolívar appeared to make amends with his vice president, but on his return to Bogotá he seemed ambivalent about the matter. On January 1, 1827, he declared amnesty for the participants in the Venezuelan rebellion. The following day, Páez acknowledged the decree and announced his fealty to the Liberator. Journeying to Venezuela later in the month, Bolívar heard stories about Páez's notorious high-handedness and the resentments the llaneros had caused, yet when he finally arrived in Caracas he joined Páez for a triumphal entry into the city. In the following days he heaped such praise on the rebellious Páez that Santander and his followers rightly concluded that Bolívar blamed them for the discord plaguing Colombia.[24]

More than anything else, the Páez rebellion made Bolívar and Santander mortal enemies. Theirs was an understandable mutual hatred. Bolívar could not abide criticism but perhaps more fundamentally he was persuaded that because he had been told so often that he was the solution to the problems of an independent Spanish America he could not understand that he might also be a part of the problem. Clearly, he did not care for Páez's ambition, privately damned his incompetence, and certainly thought him a dangerous man, but with that said he had to admit that Páez might be the only person who could keep Venezuela's fractious coteries of landowners, merchants, soldiers, and especially the grumbling ranks of pardos and blacks in check. Páez, not Bolívar, was the Venezuelan nationalist, and because Páez could exercise the strong-arm rule Bolívar believed was necessary, they were allies of a kind, at least for the time being. And if Páez refused to knuckle under to the pretentious constitutionalists in Bogotá, he would at least obey his old chief, the Liberator. After all, as Bolívar had made clear in the Angostura Address and oft repeated, Venezuelans were not yet ready for democracy. Not even dictatorship, he ruefully acknowledged to Santander before setting out for Caracas, could save Colombia. And as the English often said, neither laws or constitutions would instill a devotion to liberty among Spanish Americans. "Indians will be Indians; llaneros, llaneros; and lawyers, connivers. . . . [W]e cannot save this New World from the anarchy whose jaws are already open to devour it."[25] At this point he even mused about reviving the War to the Death decree, only this time where would he draw the line about who would be spared and who would be killed?

Bolívar remained in Caracas for six months, exhausting his energies in trying to manage a virtually bankrupt regime and daily confronting a litany of complaints from unpaid soldiers and angry pardos and former slaves. As if these problems were not enough, he got word that in Lima the Colombian troops had mutinied against their Venezuelan officers and set out for home, where news of their doings had heartened the growing anti-Bolívar movement in Bogotá. Luckily, Manuela escaped an almost certain imprisonment when she hastily packed a few belongings and Bolívar's papers and scurried north. In July, he set out for Bogotá, a trip made necessary for two reasons, one of them personal. One month into the Caracas sojourn, he had renounced the presidency of Colombia, but in June he received news that the Colombian congress had refused to accept his resignation and demanded his return to the capital to take an official oath. By then, of course, it was clear to him that there would be a showdown with Santander, perhaps a violent one. In the end, the confrontation turned out to be a battle of words: Santander publicly fumed about the Liberator's vendetta politics, but Bolívar had an army to back him up.

In those circumstances there would be little doubt about who would emerge triumphant. Bolívar took the oath on the tenth of September in a solemn ceremony, with Santander and his gaggle of disaffected and presumably humiliated constitutionalists looking on, despising the man they had tried and failed to bring down. They might have consoled themselves with the reality that practically everywhere, from Chuquisaca to Lima to Quito and on to Bogotá and Caracas, the federated Bolivarian polity was either crumbling or defiant, which meant the end of the Federation of the Andes he had cobbled together and perhaps also the Bolivian constitution that he had seemed hell-bent on making the fundamental law wherever he could.

To read his occasional somber reactions to the growing criticism of both himself and his work is to believe that Bolívar no longer cared or seemed to care what happened to his constitutional handiwork or even the Federation of the Andes. When he learned from Santa Cruz that the Bolivians were already unhappy with the constitution he had written, he responded, "Throw it in the fire if you don't want it. I don't have an author's vanity in matters of human concern."[26]

These were not the words of someone in whom the fire of will and determination still raged. Neither did they convey the sentiment of a man willing to quit. In September 1827, taking the oath of office for the last time, Simón Bolívar resolved that he had one more battle to wage.

The Final Battle

Bolívar fought his final battle not with the royalists but with his former Creole allies, and the confrontation was as much personal as ideological or political—Bolívar versus Santander, Bolivarists versus Santanderistas, centralists versus federalists, and the most enduring division of all in Colombian history, conservatives versus liberals. Throughout Bolívar remained the center of the storm, an exhausted and frustrated warrior who at forty-two received letters acclaiming his valor and perseverance from European and North American leaders and five years later could not appear in public without hearing the derisive insult "skinny shanks." Only near the end of his life, when it was too late to make his peace with anyone save the God he had doubted, did he blame himself for the torment and troubles that brought him down.

The Páez rebellion had been an early portent of the dangers to his dream of a greater Spanish-American nation. He could reconcile himself to the likelihood that there would be no Spanish-American federation or that the Federation of the Andes might not survive. But he had poured his mind and heart into the crafting of Colombia. With the mounting criticism of his appeasement of Páez and outrage in Bogotá over some of his Caracas decrees, he was persuaded that the 1821 Cúcuta convention required fundamental revisions—among them, a life presidency—in order to shield the nation from what Bolívar perceived as the excessive power of the judicial and legislative branches. Fears that his goal was the installation of another dictatorship created a firestorm among the Santanderista liberals and roused Bolívar's followers in the capital to escalate their attacks on the vice president and his liberal faction. Tensions subsided momentarily with the election of delegates to meet at Ocaña to consider the adoption of new constitutional measures. Bolívar returned to the capital in September 1827, persuaded that his reputation and fame would be sufficient incentive to the Ocaña delegates to follow his wishes. When the liberal criticism escalated, he cracked down with an emergency decree.

Early in March 1828 came another challenge, not political but racial, led by a pardo patriot admiral, José Padilla. A nominally Bolivarian follower from Cartagena, Padilla had taken the Liberator's professions of racial equality to an ideological point of no return: neither birth nor skin color should carry any privilege or social status. Instinctively, Bolívar sympathized with the efforts of Cartagena's depressed pardos to enjoy some of the benefits of independence, but he knew only too well that to acquiesce to the demands of such movements would further alarm a fearful white Creole society. Rebuffed, a chastened Padilla scurried to the town of Ocaña and the protection of Santander.[27]

The convention was in disarray. From the onset it was clear that no compromise would be possible. Bolívar's followers rejected any measure that limited his power and threatened violence if they were thwarted. A devoted lieutenant, General Rafael Urdaneta, dispatched agents into the northern provinces to promote plans for an outright dictatorship. Bolívar himself mobilized an army to march on the capital. The sole consolation of the Santanderistas was the passage of a resolution praising Padilla for his defiance of the regime. The delegates disbanded in mid-June. A few days later, Bolívar's supporters called on him "to save the republic by assuming extraordinary powers." He accepted though with dutiful expressions of reluctance, as he desired to be "far from Colombia, far from the chaos of anarchy . . . but Providence, not intending to abandon us, inspired the people of this capital with what they believed to be the only means of salvation."[28]

He now viewed himself as more than a liberator. He was a savior of the "people" and was not going to share power with anybody. But in accepting this role, and doing so in the manner he had chosen, he had effectively if not intentionally turned his back on his people by birth and those who in the aftermath of the failed convention opposed his "tyranny" and called for armed resistance. As was his wont, Bolívar took this challenge personally. He undermined Santander by abolishing the vice presidency, offering as consolation the appointment of minister to the United States. Criticism now came from virtually every social sector of the capital and even from some of his presumably steadfast friends, men increasingly critical of Manuela's influence on him. In response, Bolívar became more resolute in pushing through his reforms, though now he grounded his arguments for their passage not in Enlightenment thought but in religious tradition. Some of his enemies now wished him dead, and there were enough of them to do something about it.

The assassins struck on September 25, 1828, a date as memorable in Colombian and Venezuelan history as April 14, 1865, or November 22, 1963, in the history of the United States. There were perhaps as many as 150 conspirators—mostly Santanderistas, law students from the university, and young lawyers—who had the professed support of the commander of the local military brigade and a goodly number of his troops. The assassins' slogan was "Death to tyranny and long live General Santander." Unfortunately for the conspirators, Bolívar had sufficient warning of the impending danger, although he neglected to take any special precautions. He had survived early assassination attempts, and once more he avoided death when Manuela cleverly abetted his escape. The following day he appeared in the central plaza of Bogotá to be saluted by the military garrison and enjoy the applause from the gathering of well-wishers.[29]

Bolívar did not fear death, but the attempt on his life devastated him emotionally. His first impulse was to resign, but his supporters talked him out of such a move. Their vengeance against the conspirators surpassed that of Bolívar. Under the retributive justice of General Urdaneta, fourteen people of varying degrees of guilt were condemned and executed. One, the pardo Padillo, bore no responsibility for the assault on the Liberator's life but received a death sentence. Santander, who may have approved but against whom there was no compelling evidence of culpability, was sentenced to death as well, but he escaped execution when Bolívar pardoned him. In yet another instance during his career, Bolívar had drawn a color line. He spared the white Creole but not the pardo.

In the aftermath he grew noticeably more depressed, and as his dependence on the military and the church increased, his grip on the federated Colombian artifice weakened and then collapsed altogether. Throughout the remainder of 1828 and in all of 1829 there were intermittent challenges to his authority—in the southwestern department of New Granada; in Ecuador, where a Peruvian assault on Guayaquil prompted him to undertake an arduous journey to assist Sucre in repelling the attack; and the formal secession of Venezuela from Colombia. Perhaps the most embarrassing incident for his international reputation and particularly for his reputation among U.S. leaders came from the inept plotting of several members of his cabinet to arrange for a European prince to succeed him as monarch. In the recounting of these and less noted episodes in his last years in the cornucopia of Bolivariana, we have a wealth of commentary to serve as evidence for those who doggedly persist in framing the record and legacy of the man in either celebratory or defamatory terms. Among the most quoted phrases are his allegedly anti-imperialist warning about a United States "destined by Providence to plague America with miseries in the name of liberty" or the lament that "America is ungovernable. Those who serve a revolution plough the sea." Yet while Bolívar scribbled these phrases about the deplorable condition of independent Spanish America, the General Consul of Colombia in the United States expressed the sentiment that the "people, terrified and on the very brink of the precipice into which they were to be plunged, turned their eyes towards the only man who could save them."[30]

Too often overlooked are subtle clues and phrases in which Bolívar expressed his thoughts during the final eighteen months of his life, from mid-June 1829 to December 1830, a time when he realized that death would come either from another attempt on his life or the physical ailment daily sapping his strength. He wanted only to rid himself of his political burdens and personal demons and, like Washington, go home to die. He persisted in looking at what was occurring throughout Spanish America in personal or apocalyptic terms and sometimes both. On July 11, 1829, he wrote from Guayaquil that the Peruvian attack was an unjust war "against us." Elsewhere in the continent—in Buenos Aires, Chile, and Mexico, which "offers no hope of survival"—disorder and uncertainty convulsed society. Colombia held out some hope but only with "some sort of organization and if I am at last to be left in peace."[31]

Two days later, he poured out his anger to his minister of foreign affairs, Estanislao Vergara. The liberated republics were sinking into disorder and insecurity, fated "to destroy [themselves] and become the slave of Europe. . . . No one can hold this revolution in check." The only hope for avoiding civil war if he relinquished power was a lifetime president and hereditary senate. Those who called for a monarch as his successor were deluded, he wrote, because the insecurity, national debt, poverty, and hostility of the lower classes would be insurmountable obstacles. Where would they find a suitable European candidate willing to take on the task of resolving these problems? In the end, he felt mostly disgust "with the acts of ingratitude and the crimes that are daily committed against me." And for those who applauded his dictatorship as the rescue of the nation from chaos, he had a sobering warning: "A country that depends on the life of one man runs a risk as great as if its future were daily staked upon the cast of a die."[32]

A few weeks later, responding to a disheartening letter from Joaquín Mosquera about continuing political turmoil in Bogotá, Bolívar rendered what he believed was a confession and a pledge to mend his ways. If the anticipated "Admirable Congress" acknowledged the will of the people and divided Colombia, so be it. His enemies had "quieted down," so he now no longer felt the need to destroy them. Must they now ask that he "die upon the cross"? He added, "[W]ere it only a cross, I could suffer it with endurance as the last of my agonies. Christ endured thirty-three years of this mortal life; mine has extended over forty-six. But then I am no impassive deity; if I were, I could bear up through all eternity."[33]

Bolívar returned to Bogotá on January 15, 1830. Four days later, the Admirable Congress formally convened to address the central question of Colombian disunity. Delegates from Ecuador and New Granada favored the ruling regime, as Bolívar had anticipated, but the new document they produced closely resembled the admittedly flawed 1821 Cúcuta document. More seriously, Venezuela's separatism, which in retrospect might be considered a nationalist defiance, made any effort to salvage Colombian unity impossible. On March 1, Bolívar resigned. Denied permission by the Colombian congress to return to Venezuela, he commenced to dispose of most of his real and personal property in Bogotá. On April 27 he reaffirmed his decision not to return to power. Two weeks later, with the promise of a 30,000-peso annual pension, he held a tearful farewell with Manuela and a short time later boarded a river vessel for his final journey down the Magdalena River to the coast and a life in exile.[34]

Bolívar spent the majority of the final six months of his life in Cartagena, awaiting a vessel to take him to Europe or a friendly island in the Antilles. When it became apparent that he could not survive a sea journey, he made a short coastal voyage to Santa Marta and took up residence in the nearby plantation house of a Spaniard. A French doctor diagnosed the disease ravaging his body as tuberculosis. His skin had turned a sickening yellow, and he now weighed less than eighty pounds. Bad news dogged him in these final months. Under General Juan José Flores (an old ally), Ecuador had split off from Colombia and become a separate republic. His comrade and presumed heir apparent, Antonio José de Sucre, had been assassinated. A defiant Venezuelan congress had denied him permission to set foot on his native soil. He could not go home to die.

His warrior's determination and commitment revived for a few days in September when he got news that Rafael Urdaneta (his former foreign minister) had revolted against the government and plotted to restore Bolívar to power. Letters arrived from friends urging him to accept the challenge and to save Colombia from disaster. For a few weeks he fancied himself again at the head of a liberating army, then just as quickly recognized that to follow up on the appeal would be unwise and useless. "[T]o change a world is beyond a poor man's power, and since I am incapable of establishing the happiness of my country, I refuse to rule it. . . . [T]he tyrants of my country have expelled and outlawed me; thus I have no country to which I could render sacrifices."[35]

He had fought his final battle, and he was neither willing nor able to wage another. But to the end he held those contradictory beliefs that he was both the architect of the people's future and the undeserved victim of his critics and political enemies. His final proclamation to the Colombian people, dictated on December 10, served as the valedictory of a dying man:

> You have witnessed my efforts to establish liberty where tyranny once reigned. I have labored unselfishly, sacrificing my fortune and my peace of mind. When I became convinced that you distrusted my motives, I resigned my command. My enemies have played upon your credulity and destroyed what I hold most sacred—my reputation and my love of liberty. I have been the victim of my persecutors. . . . I forgive them. . . . You must all work for the supreme good of a united nation: The people, by obeying the present government in order to rid themselves of anarchy; the ministers . . . by addressing their supplications to Heaven; and the military, by unsheathing the sword to defend the guarantees of organized society. *Colombians!* My last wishes are for the happiness of our native land. If my death will help to end party strife and to promote national unity, I shall go to my grave in peace.[36]

Bolívar died one week later. If his death did little to ease party strife or bring about national unity, as he hoped, he may have been comforted in his final moments by remembering something he had scribbled more than a year earlier in response to depressing news from Joaquín Mosquera about events in Bogotá. Bolívar's reply commenced with a somber commentary about the mortality of man:

> Death is a terrible thing . . . because it also brings an end to the intelligent and the righteous whom we are wont to liken to divinity. . . . We feel grief for those who have departed, though we know life is evil. . . . [But] bereavement . . . is but a mechanical response of our instincts. . . . Reason [tells us] to rejoice, for death heals all our sorrows.[37]

In this passage he came as close as he ever would to reconciling the conflict between his heart and his mind, about the contradictions between someone whose being and purpose are intertwined with the particularities dictated by parentage and place and color and another who imagines a world where people are measured by universal values and in turn united in a common cause, a world where nation and identity are never subsumed to parentage or color or place. From the moment he had taken up the cause of independence and liberation, that had been the battle raging within him. Only in his last year of life, with the outcome yet unresolved, did he understand that in this struggle there is no finality, only the reassurance expressed in a Spanish proverb: "The greatness of a person is not what one achieves but what one is striving to achieve."

By the usual measures of human achievement, of course, this was an adage of little comfort to a dying man who not only lacked the strength to go on fighting but, quite frankly, no longer knew whom or what to fight. After the victory at Ayacucho, he had become so obsessed with his international adulation and recognition that he had forgotten what returning Roman conquerors had learned: All fame is fleeting. Such a person—and Bolívar was such a person—often becomes embittered if those who follow fail to value what the leader is striving to achieve. Their reasons may vary, but when everything is said and done, the most fundamental may not be that they do not value the goals the leader professes, but that they do not wish to pay the price of obtaining them.

~

Epilogue

In the last year of his life Bolívar dwelled more and more on the verdict of posterity. "My name already belongs to History," he reflected. "I love freedom no less than Washington and no one can deny that I have the honor of having humiliated the Spanish Lion from the Orinoco to Potosí."[1]

Bolívar's self-comparison with Washington was not inappropriate, although he had little reason to believe that in time his own name would inspire a cult in Venezuela that in its intensity and endurance would far surpass the public affection for Washington in the United States. The homage to Washington commenced a few days after the former president's death. It began as a campaign by a preacher and a printer to use the name to heal the wounds created by the increasingly bitter politics of the day. The adoration peaked at midcentury and then weakened as the first independent nation of the Americas collapsed in a sectional conflict that Washington feared might destroy the fragile union he had led. In the beginning, the central issue of the war was the nature of the union, and the most expedient means of preserving it. Within two years, the fundamental question was the price the North was willing to pay—must pay—to ensure not only victory on the battlefield but the future of the republic. Northern unionists now framed the fundamental stakes of the conflict in ways that suggested that victory called for the kind of war Bolívar—not Washington—had waged, a war of social reformation to rid the nation of slavery and the slavocracy.[2]

By the time laborers completed the final work on the monument in 1885, the intensity of public admiration for Washington had already begun to subside. In Venezuela, the cult of Bolívar has strengthened with each genera-tion. It began officially in an 1842 national celebration commemorating the return of his body to his native Caracas—without, as legend has it, the ashes of his heart. In 1874 came the erection of an equestrian statue in the Plaza Bolívar; two years later, transfer of his remains to the National Pantheon. At the end of the decade the caudillo president Antonio Guzmán Blanco ordered the publication of Daniel O'Leary's *Memorias* with the purpose of exalting Venezuela's greatest hero. In 1883, Venezuelans observed the cen-tenary of Bolívar's birth with celebrations, speeches, and the erection of still more statues. A public subscription campaign enabled the government to acquire Bolívar's house in 1912 and converted it into an archive and gallery, which opened in 1921. In the following decade, the Bolivarian Society of Venezuela became a national institution, committed to protecting the repu-tation and glory of the Liberator. At the bicentenary of his birth in 1983, Venezuelan soldiers, government officials, academics, business leaders, and artists lauded the Liberator in meetings, social gatherings, and publications.

Over more than two centuries, then, in a country without a glorious prehistory or colonial experience equal to that of Mexico or Peru, the name Bolívar has evoked passions and images that no other Venezuelan and—with the possible exceptions of Fidel Castro and Ernesto "Che" Guevara—no Latin American figure could touch. With every generation in Venezuela's often troubled history, the cult has strengthened and found adherents among both dictators and democrats, each seeking in the words and deeds of the man an answer to the continuing challenge of a nation striving to assume what Bolívar believed was its rightful place in the transatlantic world of the revolutionary age.

At a different level of Venezuelan society, the debates about the man and his legacy are sometimes more critical. Not surprisingly, Bolívar's own words and certainly his behavior provide ample evidence for a modern gen-eration of Venezuelans to conclude that his occasionally uncompromising judgments about federated governance, the imperative of a strong executive, and the woeful preparation of Venezuelans to assume civic responsibility, among other pronouncements, constituted a mandate not for democracy but for dictatorship. Further, his warnings about pardocracia—rule by people of color—and his willingness to use power to deny their demands for racial equality suggest that he was less a vindicator of popular rule than a leader whose professions of democracy and equality must always be measured against his recourse to dictatorial power. So strong is the cult's reach, however, that when critics rightly observe that Venezuelans declared the Liberator persona non grata and that José Antonio Páez—not Bolívar—is the "father" of Venezuela, the response is accusation that because of their denial of a homeland to Bolívar, Venezuelans committed parricide and for their punishment had to endure 150 years of misery and tyranny.

The Bolivarian legacy in New Granada followed a different pattern. His tolerance of the Páez rebellion and his attempt to impose the Bolivian constitution deeply divided the New Granadan political and social elites. One group remained committed to the Liberator, espousing his calls for a leader who would maintain social order and hierarchy. A second, identified largely with Santander, reaffirmed the liberal credos of individual liberty and democracy. Although the political lineage is imprecise, these divisions, respectively, evolved into the Conservative and Liberal parties that dominated Colombian political culture into the late twentieth century.

Critics of the Bolivarian cult point out that a nation striving to achieve social justice and responsible government should look to themselves to address their problems and not to a savior. If they stake their historical capital on Bolívar and what they believe he stood for, they place their own future in jeopardy. Bolívar himself would have endorsed this judgment. In his January 20, 1830, message to the "Admirable Congress," he wrote, "Fellow citizens, prove yourselves worthy of representing a free people by banishing the belief that I am indispensable to the Republic. If any one man were indispensable to the survival of a state, that state should not, and in the end could not, exist."[3]

With these words he expressed sentiments not unlike those written by George Washington in his Farewell Address, which is remembered mostly for his warnings against "entangling alliances" and the threat to national unity caused by the factionalism and bitterness he saw in the early republic. Where they differed lay in Washington's highlight of his unworthiness for the office of president, an unusual comment for a man who, Cincinnatus-like, was called into service over and over again. But what both were really declaring was the same belief: You will have to go on without me. Washington knew he could never survive a third term. He wished to close his life in the role dearest to him—that of a Virginia farmer and gentleman. Bolívar doubtless sensed he would not survive a long sea journey, and he was forbidden to return to his native Venezuela. Certainly, several of Bolívar's oft-quoted letters in the final year of his life express a deeper pessimism than those of Washington (who was also subjected to scathing attacks on his character), but there is no doubting the common desire for closure that inspired both men.

Washington found that closure, both in his own mind and in that of the public who after his death adulated his memory, often in exaggerated and implausible accounts of his life. If we are to believe Bolívar's oft-quoted lament that "those who serve a revolution plough the sea" and that "America is ungovernable," Bolívar regarded his life and career as a failure. Washington departed power because he was no longer needed; Bolívar, because he was no longer wanted. Why that is the case requires a closer look at three critical factors about their lives and the revolutions with which they are identified.

The first factor relates to their character and leadership abilities. Washington commanded a patriot army, but he never became a revolutionary, a dictator, or a liberator. As a Virginia patrician who modeled his behavior on that of a Roman statesman, he could easily have fitted into the country Whig aristocracy of eighteenth-century England. He became a rebel because he believed British economic policy was inefficient and made him and his fellow patrician slaveholders perpetual debtors. His notion of the development of the "inland empire" (the trans-Appalachian west) acquired with the victory over France in 1763 was distinctively that of a Virginian developer. He believed that the only way to vindicate the rights of overseas British lay in fighting. He was the only person to appear at the Second Continental Congress dressed in his Virginia militia uniform. At the end of the war, John Adams noted, the veneration accorded the man reached almost superstitious levels, and as public concerns about the future of the country grew in the postwar years, Washington became the symbol of someone who combined the stability identified with monarchy coupled with the promise of republican liberty.[4]

Bolívar's career, as we have seen, followed the path of rebel, revolutionary, liberator, and dictator. It is arguable that these were choices of circumstance and necessity rather than the proverbial search for glory or an insatiable desire for power, and that Bolívar genuinely believed that he was the guarantor of the people's freedom. In his last years in power, he disavowed the title of monarch that could have been his, yet even in this gesture of self-denial he was certainly mindful of the possibility of assassination had he taken on that role. In his military campaigns, his entry into liberated cities often inspired celebrations and festivities. Although he often dismissed the notion that his public demeanor on these occasions reminded some of a Napoleonic posturing, he certainly understood the need to identify the independence struggle with the creation of a secular patriotic culture in order to instill a sense of belonging and participation. But one could just as easily maintain that his character and ambition—his sheer will to command—were equally powerful incentives. More than other patriot leaders, he shamelessly promoted himself as moral arbiter of an idealized society and looked upon himself as another Moses, conveying the rule of law, and as the agent of Providence, which, he wrote, "has destined me to become the liberator of the oppressed peoples, [but] I will never be the conqueror of a single village."[5]

The second critical factor involves the multiple theaters of war and how the sometimes starkly varied character of each affected wartime strategies. In each of the three revolutions in the Americas (including that in Saint-Domingue) the dynamics of the conflict were different, and that reality had a powerful impact on the way the leaders of these struggles shaped their strategies and tactics. Had the British chosen to begin the war in the southern colonies instead of the eastern (i.e., New York and New England) colonies, I believe, it would have affected the outcome if not assuring a British victory. The strong sentiments for independence from Virginia into New York and New England were not so prevalent in the southern colonies, where resentments against the plantation and merchant elites inspired strong royalist feelings. The war in the southern colonies was a guerrilla war, not nearly so savage as that in Venezuela, of course, but displaying the ambivalence of guerrilla conflicts—an infuriatingly complicated struggle with no precise patterns. By the time the British shifted their strategy and launched their southern campaign, it was too late.

The war in the Bolivarian theater, particularly in Venezuela, would have rivaled in its carnage and destruction (if not in numbers of dead on the battlefield) and certainly in its numbing impact on the populace some of the battles of World War I. Even critics of Bolívar pause to pay at least minimal homage to his leadership and skill in the Venezuelan campaign, from his ability to obtain aid from Haiti to his calculated decision to shift his strategy from retaking the cities and taking the war into the countryside and mobilizing what was essentially a new army of slaves, pardos, and country people into a liberating force. The resolve Bolívar displayed in the two most critical years of the Venezuelan campaign—1817 and 1818—was even more remarkable when considered against the backdrop of the conflict in Venezuela from 1810 until his second exile in 1815. He did learn from the experience, certainly, and, as his analysis in the Jamaica Letter revealed, he was now capable of articulating the worthiness of the patriot and identifying to skeptical British (and U.S.) leaders his resolve to continue the fight.

His resolution was not the fundamental problem. He was a montage of contradictions. He condemned the separatist factions that threatened Colombian unity, but when his old Venezuelan comrade Páez led a secessionist movement, Bolívar forgave him and in turn condemned those (including Santander) who reminded him Páez's actions were unconstitutional if not treasonous. Few denied his leadership qualities, but his arguments for doing something were occasionally unsettling to his Creole allies. The nation must be unified; Venezuelans (and by implication, all Spanish Americans) were a mixed-race people; their diversity required firm and enlightened guidance from above— what he called the "moral power." No nation that aspires to greatness should tolerate slavery; we must arm the slaves to achieve victory; if we do not, they will survive and we will perish. For a leader with an undeniably grand vision for an independent Spanish America—one that he brilliantly articulated—he harbored morbidly depressing thoughts about the future.

That is perhaps understandable, it can be argued, if we look at the character of the war in Venezuela. A more persuasive explanation for his increasingly pessimistic view of the future lay in the fear—a fear even more prevalent among some of his allies—that the means he advocated for achieving unity would imperil the Creole social structure he professed to preserve. In the last years of his life, the instability and disequilibrium prompted Bolívar to become more conservative and to look with nostalgia at what others remembered as the order of the colonial era. Yet he could never reconcile the contradictory emotions that raged within him—his belief that a new political order could be founded on obedience from the masses and not force and his parallel hope that the elite would ultimately come to their senses and reconcile their differences in order to preserve social harmony.[6]

The third and, I believe, most critical factor lay in Bolívar's obsession with race and color and their effect on the war and the new republics. Even as he achieved the goal of forging unity in the creation of the union with New Granada in 1819 (and the addition of Quito in 1822) to form Colombia, he began to express his reservations that the union would survive the localism and racial diversity that he believed constituted a debilitating impediment. In 1821, when the tide of war was clearly turning in the favor of the patriot cause, he wrote despondently that Colombia was an "astonishing chaos of *patriots, royalists, egoists, blancos, pardos, Venezuelans, Cundinamarcans* [the province dominated by Santafé de Bogotá], *centralists, republicans, aristocrats, good and bad*." Eight years later, as the political crisis in Colombia deepened, he blamed the tensions raging throughout the capital on the prejudices of others. "We shall always be of reprehensible birth: Venezuelan and white," he wrote. "Guilty of this offense, we can never rule in these regions."[7]

In his reasons for taking up the sword against Spain and in his code of leadership, Bolívar was fundamentally different from Washington. Bolívar's war was personal. He wanted revenge. The memory of a Spain that had nurtured obedience, a sense of community, religious faith, and goodwill had vanished in the horror of the counterrevolution. "We are threatened with the fear of death, dishonor, and every harm," he wrote in the Jamaica Letter, "[and] there is nothing we have not suffered at the hands of that unnatural stepmother—Spain."[8]

Bolívar hated Spain not only for its arguably oppressive colonial policy, but for what it had made him and his people, a people born of the same mother but with fathers who were "foreigners" because they were of "different blood." Bolívar had perhaps a dozen reasons to justify his insistence that independence offered the only lasting assurance that Venezuelans and New Granadans and other Spanish Americans would attain their goals—international respect, self-determination, and the liberties identified with republican government. And he may have had a justifiable suspicion that despite the promises of perhaps the most democratic document of the revolutionary age—the 1812 liberal constitution of Cádiz—that Spanish liberals would never accept Spanish Americans as equals. But he could never overcome his blind hatred of a Spain that had "ceased to be European because of her African blood, her institutions, and her character."[9]

The often unspoken but generally acknowledged curse of the age for those who aspired to public social acceptance was illegitimacy of birth. Affirmation of legitimacy, after all, lay behind the "certificates of whiteness" that had so outraged Venezuelan whites. What Bolívar was implying in this damnation of Spain's "betrayal" of its European heritage, I believe, was a doubt about the legitimacy of Venezuelans and other Spanish Americans, whom he identified as a "mixed species" of people. This was a damning indictment from a man who called a Cuban black woman "father," a statement that must be measured against Bolívar's affirmation of inclusiveness regardless of color, for it suggests that for him the character and especially the color of a people are more important than the kind of government they live under. Put differently, his oft-cited observation that the laws and government of a people must take their form and inspiration from within the nation and not from an alien or foreign source presumes that he believed the people were ready or over time could be prepared for that task, when in fact he believed they could never be readied because of the indelible "stain" of Africa in their past. In word and deed, Bolívar ably defended the legitimacy of revolution, but his comments that Venezuelans (and Spanish Americans generally) were a mixed species—a people with the same mother but with different fathers "in origin and blood"—denoted illegitimacy of birth.

He was not alone in his focus on the issue of color not class as the complicating factor in governance and the preservation of the union. Already, some European and U.S. contemporaries attributed the Spanish-American condition in the aftermath of independence to the difficulty of making virtuous citizens out of a polyglot society with people of different color and experiences and particularly different beliefs about the meaning and purpose of revolution. Their solution, often, was a restoration of monarchy. Bolívar indicted the Spanish for three hundred years of tyranny, which effectively denied Spanish Americans any meaningful preparation for carrying out their civic obligations. Certainly, the institutions of liberal republican governance did take root, but the ideals of inclusion of all social groups and popular sovereignty, to continue the modern critique, constitute a fundamental requirement for nationhood.[10]

Contemporary leaders, however, might voice such sentiments as a way of mobilizing alienated or marginalized peoples or even slaves in an army. (George Washington, for example, found these soldiers far more reliable than the hallowed militias of American revolutionary lore.) The issue of their inclusion in the aftermath of the war was another matter. Beyond the issue of slave revolt, the problem most contemporary revolutionary leaders perceived, understandably so, was the demands placed upon them by alienated or marginalized groups of people. It was possible to respond with political rewards, to redefine who was white, to equate "whiteness" with progress, to expand civil liberties, and so on. Viewed through the hemispheric prism, the meaning of revolutionary-era words and ideas and particularly the "color question" assume a different meaning, and Bolívar's place in this configuration appears different as well. He was committed to the idea of racial equality but fearful of a society in which unity and nation would be subordinate to color or, more frightening, where neither color nor parentage mattered. There was little in the U.S. experience with slavery and incorporation of people of color that offered much guidance to Bolívar.

Questions of incorporation of people of color were more troublesome issues for the new republics cropping up in the Americas than for the monarchies they replaced. There had to be some variation of a republican social compact and a tacit recognition by leaders who appealed to the people that there would have to be a pecking order of who mattered more and who got more, and in this revolutionary dialectic of humans as moral and ethical beings on the one side and consumers and producers on the other, there would be a color line. The issue was further complicated by the Haitian revolution and the choices made by the Haitian slaves. To mobilize this "revolution from below," Haitian leaders had presumed that with the end of slavery it would be possible to maintain the plantation economy with a labor system that was coercive but did permit the former slaves to share in the profits. The former slaves consistently rejected this option in favor of small plots. For the freed Haitian slave, freedom was the Sunday market and progress was a hectare or so of land.

Bolívar's relevance lay in his apprehension that the incorporation of former slaves and people of color into the nation and the parallel grant of the full blessings of citizenship might not be enough. Toward the end of his career, he lamented more than once about the possible consequences of the pardos' insistence on absolute equality and what others expressed as unconditional freedom. The benefactor can more easily expand the benefits of freedom, liberty, and equality when those aggrieved people accept a definition of what is meant by the word. And he understood that those libertos and pardos in the liberating army he commanded felt and thought differently about those words than he did. He sympathized with them, knew that victory could not be attained without them, and in his more somber moments thought them more deserving than his patriot allies who feared what they might do once the fighting stopped.

This was the Bolívar dilemma. Too late, he recognized that revolution does not resolve but complicates the social question and that reform is a palliative and not a cure. He never accepted the inherent and irreconcilable conflict between the European liberal adulation of universal truths and the realities identified with place and circumstance and ethnicity and color. At bottom, however, he was more realistic than a generation of U.S. leaders who surmised that they could chart a far less risky plan for the peace and prosperity of the nation and the nurturing of a vibrant political culture than what they saw and feared in Bolívar's conception for his "America." This was a judgment presumably validated in the late 1830s by Alexis de Tocqueville in his classic survey of the U.S. social landscape, *Democracy in America*, and the spirit of young America and its self-proclaimed providential mission. The Venezuelan statesman Fermín Toro expressed a more sanguine assessment about the relevance of the American revolution: "There is no parallel between North and South America," he wrote. "In the English colonies there was no real revolution, no change in ideas, nor moral conquests, nor access to new political and philosophical doctrines."[11]

Those Latin Americans pondering the continental implications of the war with Mexico, the ambitious commercial expansion of U.S. diplomacy in the Caribbean and Central America in the 1850s, and the brief reign of William Walker in Nicaragua remembered Bolívar's warnings about a nation threatening the liberty of others in the name of freedom. In 1848 and 1856, several Latin American governments convened in Lima and Santiago, respectively, to assess these threats. The collapse of the American democracy into a savage civil war in 1861 served as a reminder of Bolívar's somber conclusions about the inherent weaknesses of federalist structures of government, the need for a strong executive, and his belief that slavery was incompatible with a free society. And the experience of free blacks and free persons of color in the slave states of the United States placed them in a category of caste. With their sacrifices and those of slaves who fled to the Union lines and joined up, the union was preserved. But in the years after the war the short-lived hope of black equality succumbed to a resurgent white supremacy. In the United States, Venezuela, and throughout Latin America, the revolutionary hope of human rights suffered as political leaders and even social scientists accepted the notion that progress depended on the "whitening" of society.

The U.S. Civil War and the reconstruction that followed was the final drama of the American Revolution. For Spanish Americans, the last battle of the war of independence was the long struggle for Cuban independence, which entered its last violent stage in 1895. That war found its voice in José Martí, the Cuban essayist, poet, and revolutionary. Martí faulted Bolívar for his failure to recognize that his power was but a temporary grant. But he lauded Bolívar's almost spiritual commitment to freedom, continental solidarity, and his belief that revolutions must bring about a social reformation. In a symbolic way, Martí wrote, the revolutionary cause of Cuba Libre in the late nineteenth century—to end the debilitating rule of Spain over Cuba and Puerto Rico—would also reconcile the persistent hatreds and fears among white, black, and colored peoples on the island. Only independence through armed struggle—not autonomy within the Spanish empire nor U.S. dominion—would provide the opportunity for Cubans to realize what Martí perceived as the fulfillment of a Bolivarian dream. "His zenith," Martí wrote, "was our continent's finest hour."[12]

Those hopes perished before a young and vigorous U.S. government that plunged into a war with Spain, in part out of long-standing fears of chaotic conditions brought on by the war in Cuba but frankly to prevent the triumph of a Cuban revolution in which people of color would share power if not dominate. In a brief but decisive conflict with Spain, U.S. military leaders often invoked rhetoric that Bolívar himself had used, avowing that their cause was not to enslave but to liberate Cuba, Puerto Rico, and the Philippines from four centuries of Spanish misrule. Within a brief span, the final outposts of Spanish rule passed from one empire to another, but not without protest and, in the case of the Philippines, the suppression of a Filipino rebellion by methods as savage as any royalists had employed in Venezuela and New Granada in their war against Spanish-American patriots. In this uneasy transition, U.S. leaders debated the issue of territoriality and ultimately statehood but concluded that to identify Cuba and Puerto Rico as territories and permit the constitutional transition to statehood would mean incorporation of peoples of color. The resolution was the status of unincorporated territories in order to distinguish between those possessions placed on the path toward statehood (Hawaii and Alaska) and those left permanently in an ambivalent status. Bolívar would have understood that decision but correctly remarked that it would not stand the test of time.[13]

In these years, as the United States began to claim the identity of America, Venezuela persisted in playing a defiant role in hemispheric affairs. Until the war with Spain, Venezuelan leaders had alternately sympathized with the Monroe Doctrine and just as quickly expressed regret about U.S. pretensions to dominate the hemisphere. In 1889, when U.S. Secretary of State James G. Blaine proposed a U.S. model for hemispheric unity, Argentina and Chile, not Venezuela, led the charge to emasculate the proposal. A decade later, Cipriano Castro, a Venezuelan liberal and Bolívar admirer, clashed with local elites. When bankers refused loans to the government (then in arrears to European and U.S. creditors), an indignant Castro paraded them in the streets as enemies of the people. In 1902–1903, he infuriated the British, German, and Italian governments over a loan default. In retaliation, and believing they had President Theodore Roosevelt's blessing, they blockaded the Venezuelan coast. In the end, Roosevelt plunged into the quarrel and, by his own reckoning, compelled the Europeans to withdraw, soothing them with his famous announcement that the United States must exercise a "policing power" in the hemisphere.

Bolívar could have predicted that scenario. He would have anticipated as well what happened to Colombia in the same era. In 1846, fearful of European and especially British machinations in Central America, the Colombian government signed a treaty with an ambitious U.S. diplomat granting the United States the right to safeguard the neutrality of the transisthmian passageway across the isthmus of Panama. On a dozen occasions between 1855 and 1903, the United States landed troops on the isthmus, all in the name of safeguarding Colombian sovereignty. On the thirteenth occasion, in November 1903, following two years of frustrating negotiations over a canal treaty, the United States again intervened, this time to prevent Bogotá from putting down a revolt. A few days later, the rebels created the republic of Panama. Rafael Reyes, the Colombian leader who became president in 1904, attributed the debacle to the bitter social and ideological divisions in the nation that had precipitated the Thousand Day War in 1899. Bolívar would have understood that humiliation as well.

A century later, the cause and dreams identified with Bolívar found yet another voice, a man who is neither poet nor essayist but a professed social revolutionary and the avowed opponent of the United States in the hemisphere. In 1998 Venezuelans elected as president the llanero Hugo Chávez, a former military paratrooper officer who led a failed 1992 coup against a government mired in corruption and rightly accused of indifference to the country's social inequities. At his urging, the national congress changed the name of the country to the Bolivarian Republic of Venezuela. Chávez's intent is to transform Venezuela into a socialist alternative to the allegedly failed political and economic model of development crafted by Venezuela's traditional elites and endorsed by the United States. Restoration of the Liberator's ideals of independence, economic self-sufficiency, and his ethic of public service, Chávez has argued, will enable Venezuela to realize the alternative society of participatory democracy, civil rights, and unity inspired by a patriotic nationalism. To evoke the Bolivarian tradition in popular culture, the *chavismo* of modern Venezuela also exalts black heroes of the revolutionary era and enthusiastically promotes llanera folk music on Caracas radio stations. To reaffirm Bolívar's imprint on the nation, the preamble declares "that the Bolivarian Republic of Venezuela bases . . . its moral authority and values of freedom, equality, justice and international peace on the doctrine of Simón Bolívar, the Liberator."[14]

At the end, then, we return to where we began—the mall in Washington, DC, at the towering monument to Washington and the equestrian statue of Bolívar not far from it. Each conveys something different to the observer. To some, the monument offers reassurance of the endurance of a nation; to others, the resolve to preserve it and the prudence to know when to act and when not to. In Washington, we imagine a person of resolve and determination, a commander and president always ready yet equally reluctant to assume the roles he played.

The statue, too, can inspire multiple and sometimes conflicting emotions, of a man who breathed a passion into the revolutionary spirit of America, a purposeful and determined warrior leading the people's army of liberation to victory, or a leader so consumed by his own ambitions and the uncertainties of his own life that the only revolutionary promise he fulfilled was endless struggle. North Americans may admire his commitment and courage but consider the revolution he led, his agenda for a union of former Spanish colonies, and his program of state building as fundamentally flawed. They may also believe his manner of waging war dangerous, his exercise of political power a threat to the constitutional process, and his views on the role of people of color in politics and society as troubling if not racist. Bolívar's Venezuelan critics have made similar observations.

Before we North Americans dismiss the man and what he stood for as representative of the "other America" and alien to our experience and beliefs, we should consider our revolution, the troubled political history of the nation in the early nineteenth century, our hemispheric record in nation building, and the history of race relations in this country. In Bolívar's indictment of slavery and his willingness to incorporate people of color in the patriot army and in civil society, he anticipated what a generation of abolitionists and unionists in the United States accepted in the 1850s and 1860s. In his last years, he was often cynical and depressed about his choice of the revolutionary path, but not any more so than John Adams or Thomas Jefferson. In the militant unionist spirit of the civil war, in Theodore Roosevelt's glorification of the warrior spirit and definition of nation and nationalism, in Woodrow Wilson's conception of nation building—in these and other traits we identify as those of "our America," we see not the shadow of Washington but that of Bolívar. We see Bolívar's vision as well in the expression of America as the "last, best hope of mankind."

In the summing up, I believe, Bolívar should be measured by words scribbled in the famous Jamaica Letter of September 1815: "More than anyone, I desire to see America fashioned into the greatest nation in the world, greatest not so much by virtue of her area and wealth as by her freedom and glory."[15]

He meant Spanish America. But he belongs to our America as well. He is one of us.

~

Notes

Preface

1. Daniel Florencio O'Leary, *Bolívar and the War of Independence: Memorias del General Florencio O'Leary: Narración*, abridged ed., trans. and ed. Robert F. McEnery Jr. (Austin: University of Texas Press, 1970), 139. See also 140–42.

Chapter 1: The Preparation

1. Quoted in John Lynch, *Simón Bolívar: A Life* (New Haven: Yale University Press, 2006), 276.

2. Quoted in Augusto Mijares, *The Liberator*, trans. John Fisher (Caracas: North American Association of Venezuela, 1991), 4.

3. Quoted in Gerhard Masur, *Simón Bolívar* (Albuquerque: University of New Mexico Press, 1969; orig. pub., 1949), 21–22.

4. Quoted in George Reid Andrews, *Afro-Latin America, 1800–1900* (New York: Oxford University Press, 2004), 49.

5. Pedro M. Arcaya, *Insurrección de los negros en la serranía de Coro* (Caracas: Pan American Institute of Geography and History, 1949), 38.

6. Salvador de Madariaga, *Bolívar* (New York: Farrar, Straus, and Cudahy, 1956; orig. pub., 1952), 27, 32.

7. For a somewhat different interpretation, see Indalecio Liévano Aguirre, *Bolívar* (Madrid: Instituto de Cooperación Iberoamericana, 1983), 17.

8. Bolívar's note is quoted in Madariaga, *Bolívar*, 35; Rodríguez's, in Masur, *Simón Bolívar*, 25.

9. Federico Brito Figueroa, *Ensayo de historia social* (Caracas: Dirección de Cultura de la Universidad Central, 1960), 199–200.

10. Madariaga, *Bolívar*, 42–43.

11. Quoted in John Lynch, *The Spanish American Revolutions, 1808–1826* (New York: W.W. Norton, 1973), 300.

12. Quoted in Aquiles Echeverri M., *Bolívar y sus treinta y más mujeres* (Medellín, Colombia: Editorial Eafit, [1985]), 19.

13. Masur, *Simón Bolívar*, 29–30.

14. Madariaga, *Bolívar*, 57.

15. Quoted in Madariaga, *Bolívar*, 58.

16. Quoted in Daniel Florencio O'Leary, *Bolívar and the War of Independence: Memorias del General Daniel F. O'Leary*, abridged ed., trans. and ed. Robert F. McEnery (Austin: University of Texas Press), 16; see also Liévano Aguirre, *Bolívar*, 38.

17. Liévano Aguirre, *Bolívar*, 39; Madariaga, *Simón Bolívar*, 66.

18. Quoted in David Bushnell, ed., *El Libertador: Writings of Simón Bolívar*, trans. Frederick H. Fornoff (New York: Oxford University Press, 2003), 114.

19. Quoted in Peggy Liss, "Creoles, the North American Example," in Jacques Barbier and Allen J. Kuethe, eds., *The North American Role in the Spanish Imperial Economy, 1760–1819* (Manchester, U.K.: Manchester University Press, 1984), 19.

20. Mijares, *The Liberator*, 115.

21. On this point see Patrick Griffin, *American Leviathan: Empire, Nation, and Revolutionary Frontier* (New York: Hill and Wang, 2007).

22. Mijares, *The Liberator*, 116.

Chapter 2: The Rebel

1. Quoted in P. Michael McKinley, *Pre-revolutionary Caracas: Politics, Economy, and Society, 1777–1811* (Cambridge, UK: Cambridge University Press, 1985), 145.

2. Henry M. Brackenridge, *Voyage to South America, Performed by Order of the American Government, in the Years 1817 and 1818 , in the Frigate Congress* (2 vols., Baltimore: author, 1819), 2: 220.

3. Karen Racine, *Francisco de Miranda: A Transatlantic Life in the Age of Revolution* (Wilmington, DE: SR Books, 2002), 143–44.

4. For an abridged text of the Jamaica Letter, see John Lynch, ed., *Latin American Revolutions, 1808–1826: Old and New World Origins* (Norman: University of Oklahoma Press, 1944), 308–20.

5. The issue is less complicated in a commonwealth system, where there may be a unifying symbol of a monarch, but even in the British example, as Canadians know only too well, the mother country at times may sacrifice the interests of its autonomous but loyal subjects in order to resolve a dispute with an independent government. The best illustration of the deceptiveness of autonomy in the U.S. system is Puerto Rico, whose people became citizens in 1917 but did not enjoy the full benefits of citizenship. At midcentury, after years of protest, Puerto Rico became a "free asso-

ciated state," enjoying the right to control of its internal affairs as well as the right to continue what is called a commonwealth, become a state, or choose independence. The reality, however, is that the island remained subject to the governance of the U.S. Congress.

6. The instructions are in Simón Bolívar, *Selected Writings of Bolívar*, ed. Harold A. Bierck Jr., trans. Lewis Bertrand, comp. Vicente Lecuna (2 vols., New York: Banco de Venezuela, 1951), 1:3–4.

7. Jose Luis Busaniche, *Bolívar visto por sus contemporáneos* (Mexico City: Fondo de Cultura Económica, 1960), 19–21; Antonio Cussen, *Bello and Bolívar: Poetry and Politics in the Spanish American Revolution* (Cambridge, UK: Cambridge University Press, 1992), 32–33.

8. See Cussen, *Bello and Bolívar*, 23–26.

9. Racine, *Miranda*, 200–208.

10. Quoted in Lester D. Langley, *The Americas in the Age of Revolution, 1750–1850* (New Haven: Yale University Press, 1996), 175–76.

11. Bolívar's speech is quoted in *Selected Writings of Bolívar*, 1:5; Busaniche, *Bolívar*, 22. See also Gerhard Masur, *Simón Bolívar* (Albuquerque: University of New Mexico Press, 1969; orig. pub., 1949), 82–89.

12. Daniel Florencio O'Leary, *Bolívar and the War of Independence: Memorias del General Daniel F. O'Leary*, abridged ed., trans. and ed. Robert F. McEnery (Austin: University of Texas Press), 2.

13. See Richard W. Slatta and Jane Lucas DeGrummond, *Simón Bolívar's Quest for Glory* (College Station: Texas A&M University Press, 2003), 49–51.

14. Augusto Mijares, *The Liberator*, trans. John Fisher (Caracas: North American Association of Venezuela, 1991), 202. The story about Bolívar's heroics is retold in Eduardo Galeano, *Memory of Fire*, vol. 2, *Faces and Masks*, trans. Cedric Belfrage (New York: W.W. Norton, 1984), 106–107. The U.S. Congress responded to news of the earthquake by unanimously approving the sending of five ships loaded with flour for the poorest regions of Venezuela. "This generous act," wrote the Bolivarian scholar Vicente Lecuna, "should be considered the noblest of gestures in the American continent" (*Crónica Razonada de las guerras de Bolívar*, 2nd ed. [3 vols., Caracas: Presidencia de la República, 1983], 1: xxvii).

15. Mijares, *The Liberator*, 216; Galeano, *Faces and Masks*, 107–108, citing Francisco Herrera Luque, *Boves, El Urogullo* (Caracas: Fuentes, 1973).

16. Juan Uslar Pietri, *Historia de la rebellion popular de 1814* (Caracas, 1962), 128.

17. Quoted in Masur, *Simón Bolívar*, 101.

18. Busaniche, *Bolívar*, 29; see also Masur, *Simón Bolívar*, 106.

Chapter 3: The Revolutionary

1. The distinguished historian of the independence movement in New Granada, José María Restrepo, calculated the white population at sixty percent, but he did so by lumping whites and mestizos into a single category. See David Bushnell, *The*

Making of Modern Colombia: A Nation in Spite of Itself (Berkeley: University of California Press, 1993), 293; and Indalecio Liévano Aguirre, *Bolívar* (Madrid: Instituto de Cooperación Iberamericana, 1983), 80–81.

2. Simón Bolívar, "Memorial Addressed to the Citizens of New Granada by a Citizen of Caracas," December 15, 1812, in David Bushnell, ed., *El Libertador: Writings of Simón Bolívar*, trans. Frederick H. Fornoff (New York: Oxford University Press, 2003), 4. See also Víctor Andrés Belaunde, *Bolívar and the Political Thought of the Spanish-American Revolutions* (New York: Octagon Books, 1967; orig. pub., 1938), 136–37.

3. Bolívar, "Memorial Addressed to the Citizens of New Granada," 6.

4. Bolívar, "Memorial Addressed to the Citizens of New Granada," 11; see also 8–9. For a discussion of gendered language in Bolívar's major addresses, see Catherine Davies, "Colonial Dependence and Sexual Difference: Reading for Gender in the Writings of Simón Bolívar (1783–1830)," *Feminist Review* 79 (March 2005): 6–11.

5. Quoted in Daniel Florencio O'Leary, *Bolívar and the War of Independence: Memorias del General Daniel F. O'Leary*, abridged ed., trans. and ed. Robert F. McEnery (Austin: University of Texas Press), 47. Indeed, Urdaneta remained loyal to the end. He fought with Bolívar against Boves during the first republic and served in New Granada. In 1818 Bolívar appointed him governor of Caracas. He fought in the fierce Venezuelan campaigns from 1818 until 1821. In 1826, he assumed the post of commander general of his native Zulia province, and in 1827 Bolívar assigned him the task of pacifying Venezuelans opposed to the central government in Bogotá. In the late 1820s, he became Secretary of War in the (Gran) Colombian government and in the tumultuous days after Bolívar's departure created a provisional government. Compelled to resign, he (and the remaining Venezuelan troops) departed for Venezuela. He died in 1845, while in service in Spain negotiating for recognition of Venezuelan independence.

6. Simón Bolívar, "War to the Death," in Bushnell, ed., *El Libertador*, 11516; see also Vicente Lecuna, *Crónica Razonada de las guerras de Bolívar*, 2nd ed. (3 vols., Caracas: Presidencia de la República, 1983), 5–6, 21–22, 25; and Liévano, *Bolívar*, 93.

7. Bolívar to the Political-Military Commission of the Supreme Congress of New Granada, August 8, 1813, in *Selected Writings of Bolívar*, ed. Harold A. Bierck Jr., trans. Lewis Bertrand, comp. Vicente Lecuna (2 vols., New York: Banco de Venezuela, 1951), 1: 34–35.

8. Fabio Puyo Vasco and Eugenio Gutiérrez Cely, eds., *Bolívar Día a Día* (3 vols., Bogotá: Procultura, 1983), 1: 196–97.

9. Joaquín Ricaurte, quoted in Liévano, *Bolívar*, 114; O'Leary, *Bolívar and the War of Independence*, 48–49; Augusto Mijares, *The Liberator* (Caracas: North American Association of Venezuela, 1991), 248.

10. Simón Bolívar, "Manifesto to the Nations of the World," September 20, 1813, in Bushnell, *El Libertador*, 125.

11. Jaime E. Rodríguez O, *Independence of Spanish America* (New York: Cambridge University Press, 1998), 93–97; see also Bolívar to James Cockburn, British governor of Curaçao, October 2, 1813, in *Selected Writings of Bolívar*, 1: 37–43.

12. Bolívar to Narciso Coll y Prat, February 1814, in *Selected Writings of Bolívar*, 1: 72.

13. Simón Bolívar, "Manifesto to the People of Venezuela," September 7, 1814, in *Selected Writings of Bolívar*, 1: 80–84.

14. Quoted in Gerhard Masur, *Simón Bolívar* (Albuquerque: University of New Mexico Press, 1969; orig. pub., 1949), 164.

15. Simón Bolívar, "Thoughts on the Present State of Europe, with Relation to America," June 9, 1814, in *Selected Writings of Bolívar*, 1: 77–79.

16. Quoted in Robert Remini, *Andrew Jackson and the Course of American Empire, 1767–1821* (New York: Harper & Row, 1977), 254.

17. Quoted in Masur, *Simón Bolívar*, 168.

18. In 1906, President Theodore Roosevelt called the military force he sent to Cuba to protect U.S. property and prevent Liberal insurgents from seizing power an "Army of Pacification."

19. Bolívar to President of the United Provinces of New Granada, May 8, 1815, in *Selected Writings of Bolívar*, 1: 96.

20. Bolívar to Maxwell Hyslop, May 19, 1815, in *Selected Writings of Bolívar*, 1: 98.

21. Bolívar to Luis Brión, July 16, 1815, in *Selected Writings of Bolívar*, 1: 99; Bolívar to [José Miguel Pey], President of the United Provinces of New Granada, August 22, 1815, in *Selected Writings of Bolívar*, 1: 102.

22. "Response from a South American to a Gentleman from This Island [Henry Cullen]," Kingston, September 6, 1815, in Bushnell, *El Libertador*, 13, 21.

23. *Selected Writings of Bolívar*, 1: 115.

24. Bushnell, *El Libertador*, 28.

Chapter 4: The Liberator

1. Bolívar to Santander, April 20, 1820, in *Selected Writings of Bolívar*, ed. Harold A. Bierck Jr., trans. Lewis Bertrand, comp. Vicente Lecuna (2 vols., New York: Banco de Venezuela, 1951), 1: 222.

2. Bolívar to Santander, April 20, 1820, in *Selected Writings of Bolívar*, 1: 223.

3. José de Cevallos, "Aspects of the Civil Strife of the *Castas* of Venezuela That Shall Be the Object of Improvement to Prevent Potential Ills and Unrest, 1815," in Christon I. Archer, ed., *The Wars of Independence in Spanish America* (Wilmington, DE: Scholarly Resources, 2000), 184.

4. Augusto Mijares, *The Liberator* (Caracas: North American Association of Venezuela, 1991), 319.

5. Quoted in Gerhard Masur, *Simón Bolívar* (Albuquerque: University of New Mexico Press, 1969; orig. pub., 1949), 219. The affair was yet another indicator that Bolívar would not tolerate insubordination and that his punishment for those who did could be severe. A decade later, when his old comrade Páez appeared to respond favorably to the pleas of several prominent Venezuelans who wanted to sever political bonds with Colombia, Bolívar reminded him of the penalty. "With me you have

won glory and fortune [and] you must place your every hope and trust in me. . . . General Piar opposed me and suffered defeat" (Bolívar to Páez, December 11, 1826, in *Selected Writings of Bolívar*, 2: 645–46).

6. Masur, *Simón Bolívar*, 124.

7. Jean-Jacques Rousseau, *Du Contrat Social*, ed. Ronald Grimsley (Oxford, UK: Clarendon Press, 1972), 47.

8. Richard Rush, secretary of state ad interim, to Caesar A. Rodney and John Graham, special commissioners of the United States to South America, July 18, 1817, in William R. Manning, ed., *Diplomatic Correspondence of the United States Concerning the Independence of the Latin American Nations* (3 vols., New York: Carnegie Endowment for International Peace, 1925), 44. On these issues, see also John J. Johnson, *A Hemisphere Apart: The Foundations of United States Policy toward Latin America* (Baltimore: Johns Hopkins University Press, 1990), 194–221; and the classic study by Arthur Preston Whitaker, *The United States and the Independence of Latin America, 1800–1830* (New York: Russell and Russell, 1962; orig. pub., 1941), 189–222.

9. Robert Remini, *Andrew Jackson and the Course of American Empire, 1767–1821* (New York: Harper & Row, 1977), 382.

10. Adams to Alexander Hill Everett, December 29, 1817, in Worthington C. Ford, ed., *The Writings of John Quincy Adams* (New York: Macmillan, 1916), 6: 282.

11. March 28, 1818, quoted in Henry Clay, *The Papers of Henry Clay*, vol. 2, *The Rising Statesman, 1815–1820*, ed. James F. Hopkins (Lexington: University Press of Kentucky, 1961), 551.

12. Johnson, *A Hemisphere Apart*, 81–82.

13. John Lynch, "Bolívar and the Caudillos," *Hispanic American Historical Review* (February 1983), 16–17. On the legionnaires see Alfred Hasbrouck, *Foreign Legionaries in the Liberation of Spanish South America* (New York: Octagon Books, 1969; orig. pub., 1928).

14. *Memorias del General Daniel Florencio O'Leary: Narración*, the first three volumes of a thirty-two-volume collection edited by his son, Simón Bolívar O'Leary, and published in Caracas between 1879 and 1888.

15. Bolívar, "Address Delivered at the Inauguration of the Second National Congress of Venezuela in Angostura," February 15, 1819, in *Selected Writings of Bolívar*, 1: 191–92.

16. Bolívar's comment is from Johnson, *A Hemisphere Apart*, 71; the other quotation is in "Slavery and the Missouri Question," *North American Review* 10 (January 1820): 158.

17. Bolívar to Santander, April 20, 30, 1820, in *Selected Writings of Bolívar*, 1: 222–23.

18. Quoted in George Reid Andrews, *Afro-Latin America, 1800–1900* (New York: Oxford University Press, 2004), 63.

19. Quoted in Masur, *Simón Bolívar*, 255. See also Daniel Florencio O'Leary, *Bolívar and the War of Independence: Memorias del General Daniel F. O'Leary*, abridged ed., trans. and ed. Robert F. McEnery (Austin: University of Texas Press), 144.

20. Quoted in *Recollection of a Service of Three Years during the War of Extermination in the Republics of Venezuela and Colombia. By an Officer of the Colombian Navy* (2 vols., London: Hunt and Clarke, 1828), I: 4–5. On the behavior of patriot troops see C. Brown, *Narrative of the Expedition to South America* (London: J. Booth, 1819), 97; and George Laval Chesterton, *A Narrative of the Proceedings in Venezuela . . .* (London, 1820), 66.

21. On the changing character of the war see Brian Hamnett, "Popular Insurrection and Royalist Reaction," in John Fisher, Allan J. Kuethe, and Anthony McFarlane, eds., *Reform and Insurrection in Bourbon New Granada and Peru* (Baton Rouge: LSU Press, 1990), 319–21.

22. Jaime Duarte French, *Bolívar, Libertador; Santander, Vicepresidente* (Bogotá: Nuevo Rumbo Editores, 1993), 83.

23. Quoted in John Lynch, *Caudillos in Spanish America, 1800–1850* (Oxford, UK: Oxford University Press, 1992), 101.

24. Quoted in Masur, *Simón Bolívar*, 313. Three years before, Thomas Jefferson expressed similar doubts in a letter to his former adversary but now confidant John Adams: "[T]he dangerous enemy is within their own breasts. Ignorance and superstition will chain their minds and bodies under religious and military despotism" (May 17, 1818, in *Writings of Thomas Jefferson* [20 vols., Washington, DC: Thomas Jefferson Memorial Association, 1904–1905], 15: 170).

25. Quoted in Mijares, *The Liberator*, 400.

26. September 6, 1815, in *Selected Writings of Bolívar*, 1: 105.

27. Captain Basil Hall, *Extracts from a Journal Written on the Coasts of Chili, Peru, and Mexico in the Years 1820, 1821, and 1822* (Edinburgh: A. Constable, 1824), 1: 222–23, 226.

28. Quoted in Richard W. Slatta and Jane Lucas De Grummond, *Simón Bolívar's Quest for Glory* (College Station: Texas A&M University Press, 2003), 228.

29. Indalecio Liévano Aguirre, *Bolívar* (Madrid: Instituto de Cooperación Iberamericana, 1983), 229. For a different perspective on the role of Manuela Sáenz, see Pamela S. Murray, "Of War and Politics: Reassessing Manuela Sáenz and Simón Bolívar, 1822–1830," *History Compass* 5, no. 1 (2007): 227–50.

30. Quoted in Liévano, *Bolívar*, 208.

31. Alvaro Valencia Tovar, *El ser guerrero del Libertador* (Bogotá: Instituto Colombiano de Cultura, 1980), 302. See also Liévano, *Bolívar*, 236, 240–41; and Vicente Lecuna, *Crónica razonada de las guerras de Bolívar* (3 vols., New York: Colonial Press, 1950), 3: 204–207.

Chapter 5: The Victor

1. Adams to Richard Anderson, May 27, 1823, in Worthington C. Ford, ed., *The Writings of John Quincy Adams* (7 vols., New York: Greenwood Press, 1968), 7: 466. Anderson was the first U.S. minister to Colombia.

2. Indalecio Liévano Aguirre, *Bolívar* (Madrid: Instituto de Cooperación Iberamericana, 1983), 246.

3. Quoted in Jose Luis Busaniche, *Bolívar visto por sus contemporáneos* (Mexico City: Fondo de Cultura Económica, 1960), 117. A U.S. diplomat who met Bolívar a short time later wrote a similarly complimentary description: "His whole Soul is wrapt up in the emancipation of his Country and America is that Country, all his aspirations are for its happiness" (John Prevost to Sec. of State John Quincy Adams, October 28, 1823, in William Manning, ed., *Diplomatic Correspondence of the United States Concerning the Independence of the Latin-American Nations* [3 vols., New York: Carnegie Endowment for International Peace, 1925], 1088). Page numbers in these volumes are continuous.

4. Simón Bolívar, *Cartas del Libertador*, Vicente Lecuna, ed., vols. 1–10 (Caracas: Banco de Venezuela, 1929–1930), 3: 229; Daniel Florencio O'Leary, *Bolívar and the War of Independence: Memorias del General Daniel F. O'Leary*, abridged ed., trans. and ed. Robert F. McEnery (Austin: University of Texas Press), 240–41, 248–49.

5. Bolívar to Sucre, May 24, 1823, in *Selected Writings of Bolívar*, ed. Harold A. Bierck Jr., trans. Lewis Bertrand, comp. Vicente Lecuna (2 vols., New York: Banco de Venezuela, 1951), 2: 373.

6. Quoted in Gerhard Masur, *Simón Bolívar* (Albuquerque: University of New Mexico Press, 1969; orig. pub., 1949), 375.

7. Quoted in Robert L. Scheina, *Latin America's Wars*, vol. 1, *The Age of the Caudillo, 1799–1899* (Washington, DC: Brassey's, 2003), 40; see also p. 70.

8. Bolívar to Santander, January 6–7, 1825, in *Selected Writings of Bolívar*, 2: 461.

9. Quoted in Víctor Andrés Belaunde, *Bolívar and the Political Thought of the Spanish-American Revolutions* (New York: Octagon Books, 1967; orig. pub., 1938), 225.

10. The quotations are in Simon Collier, "Nationality, Nationalism, and Supra-nationationalism," *Hispanic American Historical Review* 1 (February 1983): 49–51.

11. Vicente Lecuna, *Crónica Razonada de las Guerras de Bolívar* (3 vols., New York: Colonial Press, 1950), 3: 526.

12. "South America," *North American Review* (July 1824): 159.

13. Quoted in Arthur Preston Whitaker, *The United States and the Independence of Latin America, 1800–1830* (New York: Russell and Russell, 1962; orig. pub., 1941), 540, 542.

14. Quoted in John J. Johnson, *A Hemisphere Apart: The Foundations of United States Policy toward Latin America* (Baltimore: Johns Hopkins University Press, 1990), 11.

15. Whitaker, *United States and the Independence of Latin America*, 580–81.

16. James H. Lewis, *The American Union and the Problem of Neighborhood: The United States and the Collapse of the Spanish Empire, 1783–1829* (Chapel Hill: University of North Carolina Press, 1998), 218.

17. "South America," *North American Review* (July 1824): 162; Henry Clay, *The Papers of Henry Clay*, ed. James F. Hopkins (Lexington: University Press of Kentucky, 1961), 6: 312.

18. Bolívar to Manuela Sáenz, April 20, 1825, in *Cartas del Libertador*, 4: 315–16; Masur, *Simón Bolívar*, 399–400.

19. Quoted in D. A. Brading, *The First America: The Spanish Monarchy, Creole Patriots, and the Liberal State, 1492–1867* (Cambridge, UK: Cambridge University Press, 1991), 617–18.

20. Hiram Paulding, U.S. Navy, *Sketch of Bolívar in His Camp* (1835), quoted in David Bushnell, ed., *The Liberator Simón Bolívar: Man and Image* (New York: A. A. Knopf, 1970), 96–97; Everett to Sec. of State Henry Clay, January 27, 1827, in Manning, *Diplomatic Correspondence*, 2139–40.

21. Message to the Congress of Bolivia, May 25, 1826, *Selected Writings of Bolívar*, 2: 596.

22. Eduardo Galeano, *Faces and Masks* (New York: W.W. Norton, 1998), 130–32.

23. Bolívar to Santander, July 8, 1826, in *Selected Writings of Bolívar*, 2: 624–25.

24. Busaniche, *Bolívar*, 238–39.

25. Bolívar to Santander, November 5, 1826, in *Selected Writings of Bolívar*, 2: 641.

26. Quoted in John Lynch, *Simón Bolívar: A Life* (New Haven, CT: Yale University Press, 2006), 230.

27. Aline Helg, "Simón Bolívar and the Spectre of *Pardocracia*: José Padilla in Post-Independence Cartagena," *Journal of Latin American Studies* 35 (August 2003): 447–71.

28. Bolívar to José Fernández Madrid, Colombian Minister to England, June 28, 1828, in *Selected Writings of Bolívar*, 2: 701.

29. Fabio Puyo Vasco and Eugenio Gutiérrez Cely, eds., *Bolívar Día a Día* (3 vols., Bogotá: Procultura, 1983), 3: 470.

30. Columbian Consul General in the United States to Martin Van Buren, Secretary of State of the United States, April 16, 1829, in Manning, *Diplomatic Correspondence*, 1328. Bolívar may have intended his comment about the miseries committed in the name of liberty as a warning applicable to the designs of all the new states of America, including the United States. In any event, the new U.S. minister to Colombia, William Henry Harrison, was especially severe in his criticism of Bolívar. See Harrison to Sec. of State Martin Van Buren, May 27, 1829, in Manning, *Diplomatic Correspondence*, 1333–36.

31. Bolívar to Bruno Espinoza, July 11, 1829, in *Selected Writings of Bolívar*, 2: 722–23.

32. Bolívar to Vergara, July 13, 1829, in *Selected Writings of Bolívar*, 2: 725–26.

33. Bolívar to Joaquín Mosquera, September 3, 1829, in *Selected Writings of Bolívar*, 2: 733–34.

34. The journey and a portrait of the man in all his complexity are recounted in Gabriel García Márquez, *The General in His Labyrinth*, trans. Edith Grossman (New York: Alfred A. Knopf, 1990).

35. Quoted in Masur, *Simón Bolívar*, 484.

36. "Proclamation to the People of Colombia," December 10, 1830, in *Selected Writings of Bolívar*, 2: 765.

37. Bolívar to Joaquín Mosquera, September 3, 1829, in *Selected Writings of Bolívar*, 2: 733.

Epilogue

1. Quoted in D. A. Brading, *The First America: The Spanish Monarchy, Creole Patriots, and the Liberal State, 1492–1867* (Cambridge, UK: Cambridge University Press, 1991), 619.

2. One was Edward Everett (the other speaker at the commemoration of the Gettysburg battlefield), who in 1821 had judged that "Bolívar was no Washington" and had become absorbed and disturbed about the racial makeup of Bolívar's army and the power he exercised in the pursuit of a patriot victory. Remorseful over his old-line Whig compromises over slavery, he resigned his Massachusetts U.S. Senate seat. During the war he lectured to enthusiastic crowds in the North about the need to preserve the union at any cost.

3. Simón Bolívar, *Selected Writings of Bolívar*, ed. Harold A. Bierck Jr., trans. Lewis Bertrand, comp. Vicente Lecuna (2 vols., New York: Banco de Venezuela, 1951), 2: 754.

4. Barry Schwartz, *George Washington: The Making of an American Symbol* (New York: Free Press, 1987), 50–53.

5. Quoted in Karen Racine, "Simón Bolívar, Englishman: Elite Responsibility and Social Reform in Spanish American Independence," in David Bushnell and Lester D. Langley, eds., *Simón Bolívar: The Life and Legacy of the Liberator* (Lanham, MD: Rowman & Littlefield, 2008), 65.

6. Tulio Halperin-Donghi, *The Aftermath of Revolution in Latin America*, trans. Josephine de Bunsen (New York: Harper and Row, 1973), 131–35.

7. The two quotations are in Simon Collier, "Simón Bolívar as Political Thinker," in Bushnell and Langley, *Simón Bolívar*, 29, 30.

8. *Selected Writings of Bolívar*, 1: 105

9. *Selected Writings of Bolívar*, 1: 181.

10. John Charles Chasteen, *Americanos: Latin America's Struggle for Independence* (New York: Oxford University Press, 2008), 184–86.

11. Quoted in Judith Ewell, *Venezuela and the United States* (Athens: University of Georgia Press), 40.

12. José Martí, "Simón Bolívar," in Deborah Shnookel and Mirta Muñiz, eds., *José Martí Reader: Writings on the Americas* (New York: Ocean Press, 1999), 163.

13. He was right. In the early twenty-first century, a special task force studying the "commonwealth" status of Puerto Rico concluded that the U.S. Constitution made no provision for such an arrangement.

14. Quoted in Germán Carrera Damas, "The Hidden Legacy of Simón Bolívar," in Bushnell and Langley, *Simón Bolívar*, 65. See also Richard Gott, *In the Shadow of the Liberator: Hugo Chávez and the Transformation of Venezuela* (New York: Verso, 2000).

15. *Selected Writings of Bolívar*, 1: 115.

~

Bibliographical Note

Those looking for a more in-depth assessment of many of the issues and controversies surrounding the life of Simón Bolívar from North American, Venezuelan, and Colombian perspectives should consult the companion volume to this biography, David Bushnell and Lester D. Langley, eds., *Simón Bolívar: The Life and Legacy of the Liberator* (Lanham, MD: Rowman & Littlefield, 2008).

A bibliography of Bolivariana would require a book in itself. Most of the literature is in Spanish, and the hagiographic literature on the life of the Liberator dominates. For the general reader and student, I suggest the following biographies and collections for an introduction to his life and times.

A recent brief account of Bolívar's life is David Bushnell, *Simón Bolívar: Liberation and Disappointment* (New York: Pearson Longman, 2004), which offers a balanced although not always uncritical assessment. For a more detailed biography, see John Lynch, *Simón Bolívar: A Life* (New Haven, CT: Yale University Press, 2006), a narrative by a distinguished Latin Americanist who ably integrates Bolívar's life into the Spanish American independence movement. Gerhard Masur, *Simón Bolívar* (Albuquerque: University of New Mexico Press, 1969; orig. pub., 1948), served for many years as the standard biography in English. Both the Bushnell and Lynch biographies represent an effort to rehabilitate the art of biography among academic historians.

Bolívar was a multifaceted, controversial, and adulated figure. The closest to a balanced Venezuelan account of his life is Augusto Mijares, *El Libertador* (Caracas: Fundación Eugenio Mendoza and Fundación Shell, 1964), which is available in an English edition. The Spaniard Salvador de Madariaga scandalized Venezuelans with his *Bolívar* (New York: Pellegrini and Cudahy, 1952), which portrayed the Liberator as a schemer and opportunist. In *The General in His Labyrinth*, the famous Colombian novelist Gabriel García Márquez employs a magical narrative style to flesh out the Liberator's life through his seven-month journey down the Magdalena River in 1830.

For background on the Spanish-American wars of independence see John Lynch, *The Spanish American Revolutions, 1808–1826* (New York: W.W. Norton, 1973), which should be supplemented with more recent accounts by Jaime Rodríguez O, *The Independence of Spanish America* (New York: Cambridge University Press, 1998) and John Charles Chasteen, *Americanos: Latin America's Struggle for Independence* (New York: Oxford University Press, 2008). The most accessible English-language translation of Bolívar's voluminous correspondence is *Selected Writings of Bolívar*, ed. Harold A. Bierck Jr., trans. Lewis Bertrand, comp. Vicente Lecuna (2 vols., New York: Colonial Press, 1951), which should be supplemented with David Bushnell, ed., *El Libertador: Writings of Simón Bolívar*, trans. Frederick Fornoff (New York: Oxford University Press, 2003). No account of Bolívar's illustrious and tumultuous life would be understandable without referring to the multivolume *Memoria* of his trusted aide, Daniel O'Leary, whose narrative has been concisely edited and translated by Robert F. McNerney Jr.: *Bolívar and the War of Independence: Memorias del General Daniel Florencio O'Leary, Narración*, abridged ed. (Austin: University of Texas Press, 1970). Germán Carrera Damas, *El culto a Bolívar* (Caracas: Universidad Central de Venezuela, 1969) fundamentally reshaped Bolivarian historiography.

For the hemispheric background on the wars of independence in the Americas, see Lester D. Langley, *The Americas in the Age of Revolution, 1750–1850* (New Haven: Yale University Press, 1996); John J. Johnson, *A Hemisphere Apart: The Foundations of United States Policy toward Latin America* (Baltimore: Johns Hopkins University Press, 1990), and the classic account, Arthur P. Whitaker, *The United States and the Independence of Latin America, 1800–1830* (New York: Russell and Russell, 1962; orig. pub., 1941).

I have identified other relevant studies, including those in Spanish, in the notes.

Index

~

About the Author

Lester D. Langley grew up in Texas and earned his doctorate in U.S. foreign relations and Latin American history at the University of Kansas in 1965. Following brief teaching stints at Texas A&M University and Central Washington University, he rose from associate to research professor at the University of Georgia. Following his retirement from that institution in 2000, he held visiting professorships at the University of Texas (Austin) and Texas A&M University. He has published or edited sixteen books, principally on U.S. relations with Latin America. He is general editor of the well-received University of Georgia Press series, "The United States and the Americas." In 1996 Yale University Press published his comparative and "hemispheric" history of the wars of independence in the Americas, *The Americas in the Age of Revolution, 1750–1850*. That book and a subsequent volume (Langley and David Bushnell, eds. *Simón Bolívar: The Life and Legacy of the Liberator*) provided the inspiration for this brief biography of the most controversial figure in those struggles that convulsed the Americas in the half-century after 1776.